※※※

Heather Tosteson's *Source Notes: Seventh Decade* is a brave, unvarnished reassessment of the poet's life, an unsentimental reckoning that celebrates awe, wonder, and gratitude, while accepting and confronting remorse, betrayal, and loss. The poems in this volume express Tosteson's hard-won wisdom that "our ultimate consolation / lives inside our most inexhaustible pain." In moving poems that span continents and careen through time, she confronts generational trauma, and does not turn away from the choices she has made, or from the hard truths she has had to accept. For Tosteson, memory is both a consolation and a torment, and she braves "joy-steeped grief" while "drenched in goodness." In lyrical poems that beguile with their music, and stun with their candor, Heather Tosteson invites us to share "the ripe wild fruit of eternity."
—**Gary Young**, author of *That's What I Thought: Poems* and *New and Selected Poems*

※※※

Walt Whitman wrote in Song of Myself, "I am large, I contain multitudes." So too does Heather Tosteson. In *Source Notes*, there is an abundance of wisdom, also an abundance of pain—abuse, mental illness, misunderstandings—interwoven into luminous poems in which tree frogs and quetzals are as likely to show up as estranged relatives yearning for reconciliation. Tosteson seeks to understand them all, and when understanding proves beyond her reach, she chooses to uphold the moments of grace that shine in the darkness.
—**Kathleen Housley**, author *Firmament, Epiphanies, and The Scientific World of Karl Friedrich Bonhoeffer*

⟆⟅⟆

   In her newest collection of poetry, Heather Tosteson once again delivers an exquisitely crafted vision of existence that is simultaneously broad and intimate, beautiful and fraught, manageable (through tremendous effort) and wild. Her poems do not lie. What is reported in these pages about the solace of nature, the enlightenment of travel, family struggles, the unbreakable bond of mother and son, aging and what it means to be a citizen in our current world is suffused with awe, rage, despair and—yes!—hope. In *Source Notes: Seventh Decade*, Tosteson is writing at the top of her poetic game.
—**Kat Mead**s, author of *Dear DeeDee*

⟆⟅⟆

   Heather Tosteson's poems sail courageously across unexplored oceans of "the heartbreaking irreconcilability/ of cause and consequence." She is fierce and unflinching. "The truth grows cold," she writes, "if we don't hold it./ And we grow old/ regardless." Poem by poem, as I savored *Source Notes: Seventh Decade*, Tosteson's latest collection, I grew increasingly inspired. It's wonderful for a young poet to be bold and brave, but it's an even more miraculous feat for an artist entering her 70's. Her words are "pure fire, phosphorus white,/ burning from infancy straight/ into this very night/ in my seventh decade."
—**Lowell Jaeger**, Montana Poet Laureate 2017-2019, author of *Earth-blood & Star-Shine*

⟆⟅⟆

   In *Source Notes: Seventh Decade*, Heather Tosteson maps the inner lives of women in a way that is both mystical and deeply intellectual, keeping alive poetry's big questions of transcendence, revelation, awe, and grounded presence in the ordinary. What a large and compassionate gift to the reader, a gift from a life given to inner investigation of what it means to be a human being anchored within the tangible things of the world. As the poet says, Trust the emptiness within/ and the rain sifting gently/ through palm, jacaranda and mimosa.
—**Mary Kay Rummel**, author of *Nocturnes: Between Flesh and Stone,* poet laureate emerita of Ventura County, CA

※※※

In these meticulously-crafted poems, Heather Tosteson evocatively limns one woman's courageous and authentic journey as she revisits the past, explores and marvels at the present, and dares to imagine a bountiful future for herself and humankind across the globe. Visual art woven throughout *Source Notes: Seventh Decade* complements and enhances text that reads not only as a poignant and powerful poetry collection, but also as a compelling, narrative-driven memoir-in-short-chapters. The creativity, bravery, and wisdom of Tosteson's narrator are hard-earned, genuine, and ever-evolving. She reassures the reader, "We are never too old for rebirth"—and we believe her.
—**Janice Eidus**, author of *The Last Jewish Virgin* and *The War of the Rosens*

※※※

"I just want to make meaning of my life," writes Heather Tosteson. She does that with contemplative care in all the biographical poems in *Source Notes: Seventh Decade*. Reading them, I am reminded that everything that has happened and everything that might happen is informed by the internal narratives we, especially poets, create to make sense of life's own unfolding narrative. A life lived vividly shape-shifts over time, if we are to grow. With growth comes reckonings, evolving intimacies, reconciliations, acceptance, even redemption. I felt more grounded in my own relationship with ageing as I read these poems by a kindred spirit.
—**Felicia Mitchell**, author of *Waltzing with Horses*

※※※

Source Notes: Seventh Decade is an amazing collection. Tosteson's well-crafted poems cover a broad territory with candor and depth. I loved her honesty and straight-forward tone, conveying, at times, abstract ideas but never attempting to deceive. Her remarkable photographs, so powerful in their simplicity, contribute additional levels of meaning as well, revealing the unexpected, the 'just-out-of sight,' or what often goes unseen.
—**Diana Anhalt**, author of *Walking Backward*

SOURCE NOTES
SEVENTH DECADE

SOURCE NOTES
SEVENTH DECADE

Heather Tosteson

Wising Up Press

Wising Up Press
P.O. Box 2122
Decatur, GA 30031-2122
www.universaltable.org

Copyright © 2021 by Heather Tosteson

All rights reserved. No part of this book may be used or reproduced in any manner whatsoever without written permission, except in the case of brief quotations embodied in critical articles or reviews.

ISBN: 978-1-7324514-8-3

Catalogue-in-Publication data is on file with the Library of Congress.
LCCN: 2021931459

*Yet again—
to the two great loves of my life,
CB and TR*

TABLE OF CONTENTS

Synesthesia	*1*

I

THE SONGS ARE GONE

This Is What I Know	*6*
The Songs Are Gone	*7*
La Pregunta Sin Respuesta, Sin Fin	*8*
Climate Change	*11*
Accounting	*12*
This Is My Hate Song	*14*
When I Turn a Blind Eye	*16*
I Want to Ask Them	*17*
In These Days of Outrage	*19*

CREATING

Creating	*22*
Carry-Ons	*23*
Dismissals	*24*
If I Were to Open That Knot	*27*
Source Notes	*28*
Open Veins	*31*
Girl in the Grip of an Idea	*32*
Symbiosis	*36*
Figment	*39*
This Moment	*40*

THE SECRET SWEETNESS OF VEJEZ

Who Says	*44*
The Secret Sweetness of Vejez	*45*
Carolina Summer	*46*
I Saw the Lines	*47*
I Just Want to Lie Up Here in the Dark	*48*
Flowers on the Sand	*50*
If I Could Choose	*52*
The Wind Is Having Its Way Today	*53*
The Color of Honey	*55*
Trust the Emptiness Within	*56*

II
LETTERS TO MY SON, TWENTY YEARS A MAN

Órale, Hijo Mío	62
No Call, No Card	63
Palomas	64
Letters for My Son, Twenty Years a Man	66
Los Voladores	74
Décimas for My Son in his Fifth Decade	77
Call Waiting	80
Monteverde	83

SHAKEN BABY, FOREVER HELD

When the Light Was Waning	88
Where Story Begins	89
I Have Put My Words in Order	90
That's What I Want	91
Dialogics	93
Words That Never Know Air	94
Dangers of Public Speaking	96
Just Because	98
Russian Dolls	100
Mirror Neurons	104
Day of the Dead	107

FAMILY FEELING

Family Feeling	112
There Is A New Story Burgeoning	113
Just Like Everyone	114
Afterlife	118

III
Life in Translation

Regresaremos	128
Oaxaca, December 2014	129
Departure	136
Now Não	137
Life in Translation	138
Quem Tem Alma Não Tem Calma	141
Voices in a Sevilla Night	145
Hoarding	152
Songs for the Faint of Heart and Misaligned	154
Pura Vida	156
Penetration	164
Ways of Moving Through the World	168
Footprints in the Air	170
Entraining with the Holy	172
It Is So Hard to Leave Valparaíso	175

The Space Between Now and Never

We Write to Redeem Ourselves	178
Like a Hermit Crab, I Have Dreams	179
Totems	180
Scorpio Mothers	182
You Can't Speed Up Time	185
The Space Between Now and Never	189
Resonance	192
The Day I Took My Mother to Her New Home	196
In These Days, In This Time	198
I Don't Want to Move Anything Forward Today	199
It's Time to Start Talking	200
What If	203
All Night I Dreamt	204

Acknowledgements	207
Author	209

SYNESTHESIA

What is the sound of a true word
never said? Of our own blood returning
fully assured of its welcome?

What is the sound of this feeling
pouring out of us now like life blood
as it coagulates, dries?

What is the sound of listening
to a stranger's face? To a life story
brought into being purely
by the quality of our own hearing?

What is the sound of love
we never believed in
leaving? Holding fast?
Outlasting us?

What is the sound of a siren's song
to an ear deafened by shell shock?

What is the sound of silence
to a mind that rattles
like an empty bird cage
in a violent wind?

What is the sound of stars settling
into a new constellation that no one
as yet has the wit to see?

What is the sound of a heart,
on the far shore of terror, echoing
the melody of an ancient lullaby?

What is the sound of your being
resounding in me?

THE SONGS ARE GONE

THIS IS WHAT I KNOW

The truth grows cold
if we don't hold it.
And we grow old
regardless.

THE SONGS ARE GONE

The songs are gone.
The songs are gone
into hiding.
I must find them.

The songs are gone
into hiding like my neighbors
who won't leave their houses
for fear of thieving boys dark
as shadows, thin as blades,
or dead letters slipped decades
too late under barred front doors.

LA PREGUNTA SIN RESPUESTA, SIN FIN

El mundo da vueltas
y da vueltas, y da vueltas
y la pregunta persiste:
¿Ciclo virtuoso?
¿Ciclo vicioso?
¿En cuál estamos enredados?
La pregunta persiste,
persiste sin respuesta
siglo, tras siglo, tras siglo.

La luz se convierte en la noche,
el amor en lo odio
la libertad en la tiranía,
lo dulce en lo amargo,
la verdad en la mentira,
lo conocido en lo extraño,
la alegría en la angustia,
las risas en las lagrimas
y la esperanza en—
y la esperanza en—

El mundo da vueltas,
la luz sigue la noche, la noche sigue
la luz, primero la una, luego la otra,
sale y regresa, regresa y sale, sale, sale,
y otra vez, insaciablemente, regresa
la luz, lo mismo que el amor, la amistad,
la dulzura, la alegría y las risas . . .

Si persistimos fieles e inmóviles,
como las piedras, la tierra,
y los huesos secos,
si persistimos y levantamos nuestros ojos
al cielo, crédulos como santos y locos,
veremos, sin duda,
algo vivo, con las alas extendidas,
revoloteando
como una paloma
como un zopilote
como un espíritu santo,
algo hambriento, verdaderamente
libre, real,
fijándose en nosotros con los ojos claros
y las intenciones oscuras.

Y la pregunta insaciable revive:
¿Ciclo virtuoso?
¿Ciclo vicioso?
¿En cuál estamos enredados,
siglo, tras siglo, tras siglo?

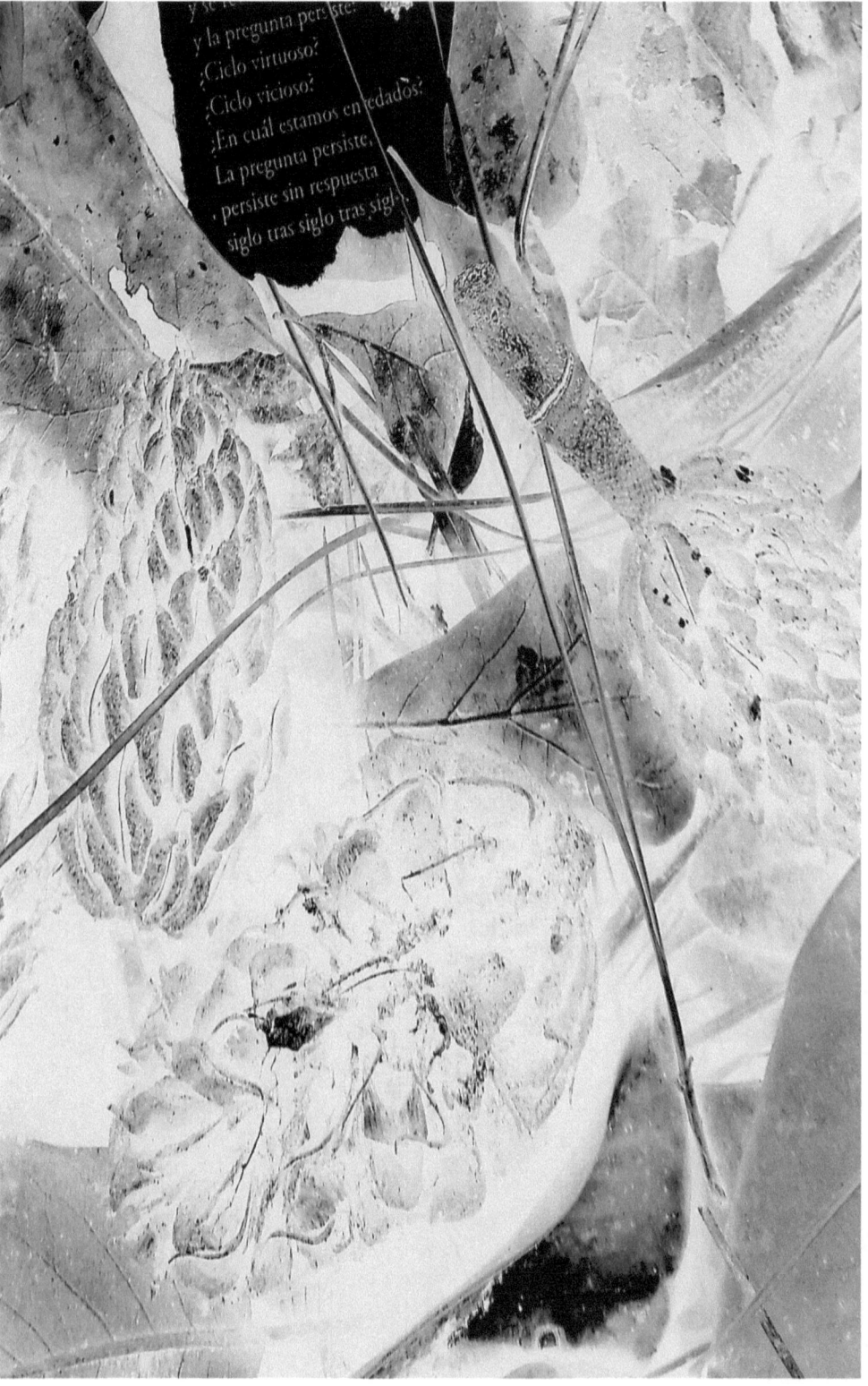

CLIMATE CHANGE

No more princes and principalities,
no more let's make America
great again, no more
frontiersmen or robber barons.
No more conspiracies or
adamantine beliefs, adamantine
grief. Just real clouds
of unknowing, real whirlwinds
that in minutes strip the trees
of all their golden leaves.

ACCOUNTING

Cardinal rustling in the tulip tree,
coyote sleeping near the creek.
Helicopters circling overhead
as if this were Watts, not
a quiet cul de sac in Georgia
where I am taking the whole day off.
A manic depressive on a short leash
feeling the bite of that tether.
I have to pull myself together.

Too many days spent imagining
my way into lives I wouldn't want to lead.
MLK, tears in his eyes, offers food
to a small child murmuring,
"It will get better by and by."
Decades later, freed from prison,
she wields a kitchen knife when she feels
short-changed of her grown son's attention.

How dare he favor his own children
when she's prepared a meal for him.
For decades she's dreamed of this moment,
of what might have been and still could be
if people just played by the rules
of her own psyche. He pushes his children
behind him, raises his hand.
"Try that and I will *do* you," she warns him.

She warns me too, eyes gleaming, voice
bright as that knife. "When I look at you
I see a business woman with an investment
in understanding but no heart, no
humanity." I feel like a spendthrift
even listening. What on earth was I thinking
to come here. She's hurt I didn't share
my own roof when she was homeless.

I pick and choose my words like precious jewels
from a plundered safe. Not cold. Not fool.
Certainly not foolhardy. Not as hopeful
as MLK. Bankrupt. Maybe that's the word I'm seeking.
No one could ever pay me enough to do this.
I envy her longer leash and reach. I want to say,
"Do you have any idea what it costs me
to get this close. *Do* you?"

Instead I say, "I'm so sorry you see me that way.
But you're right. I do want to understand."
"I know I got to you," she murmurs with a smile.
"Your face is red." Thin-skinned, *my* tell.
I take a deep breath. I know she is honoring me
with her ruthless truth. Am I free to refuse it?

THIS IS MY HATE SONG

This is my hate song.
I dare you to sing along.

I want an end
to God, guns, country
as a raison d'être,
an origin story, an end
in itself. I'm tired of men
silencing the voices of women
who question them, grabbing their
crotches under tables,
shoving their tongues into them
in elevators, and telling them
to buy a version of reality
so venial, so cruel
that it defies imagination.
My imagination.
My own rage defies my imagination.

WHEN I TURN A BLIND EYE

When I turn a blind eye
to the good you've done,
does my wrong
add another rung
just like yours
to a ladder leading
nowhere?

I WANT TO ASK THEM

I keep thinking about how the mothers
didn't want their babies, even stillborn, to decay.
How one left her newborn infant, lifeless,
in a cooler patterned with bright watermelon slices,
handle extended, in the middle of a barren field
along a busy highway, an open secret.
Another kept her stillborn home with her
for six months in her freezer.
Or the mother who, drunk, desperate,
took her whole universe—
wife and six adopted children—
with her over the cliff, so sure
no one could ever care like her.

And about those rowdy adolescent boys
with their red Make America Great Again caps,
gathered in front of the Lincoln Memorial,
high from hormones and the excitement of marching
for the right to life, for the right to extinguish
a woman's right to choose to bring them,
such primed, loose, sperm-laden canons,
into this world. How one of them,
still pumped, still plump with baby fat,
stripped off his shirt, bent his knees
to thrust out his pelvis, and jumped up and down
like any belligerent young primate inviting
someone, anyone, to tangle with him, skin to skin.

I want to ask them too, seriously,
What does love have to do with it?

IN THESE DAYS OF OUTRAGE

In these days of outrage,
vindictiveness, exhausted
invective, I feel a call
to a god with breasts
and clitoris who refuses
definition, who has a voice
deep and rich as a man's
but smooth as a slow moving river,
who sings constantly
in a language we all yearn
to remember, one that doesn't
dismember, revile or deny.
My whole body comes alive
when she enters my imagination.
I move with the ease of a young girl,
my flesh has the gravitas
of a new mother. I am *of* her.
Of this I have no doubt.

But does that mean I share her keen,
clear mind, the way she can
take us in without the baggage
so at last we realize,
naked, poor, hungry, or imprisoned,
sick or rich,
anxious, jealous, grasping,
hale in body
and harsh in heart,
as rank with success
as we are with failure, that—

we are—and always have been—
fully loved,
we are— and always have been—
enough.

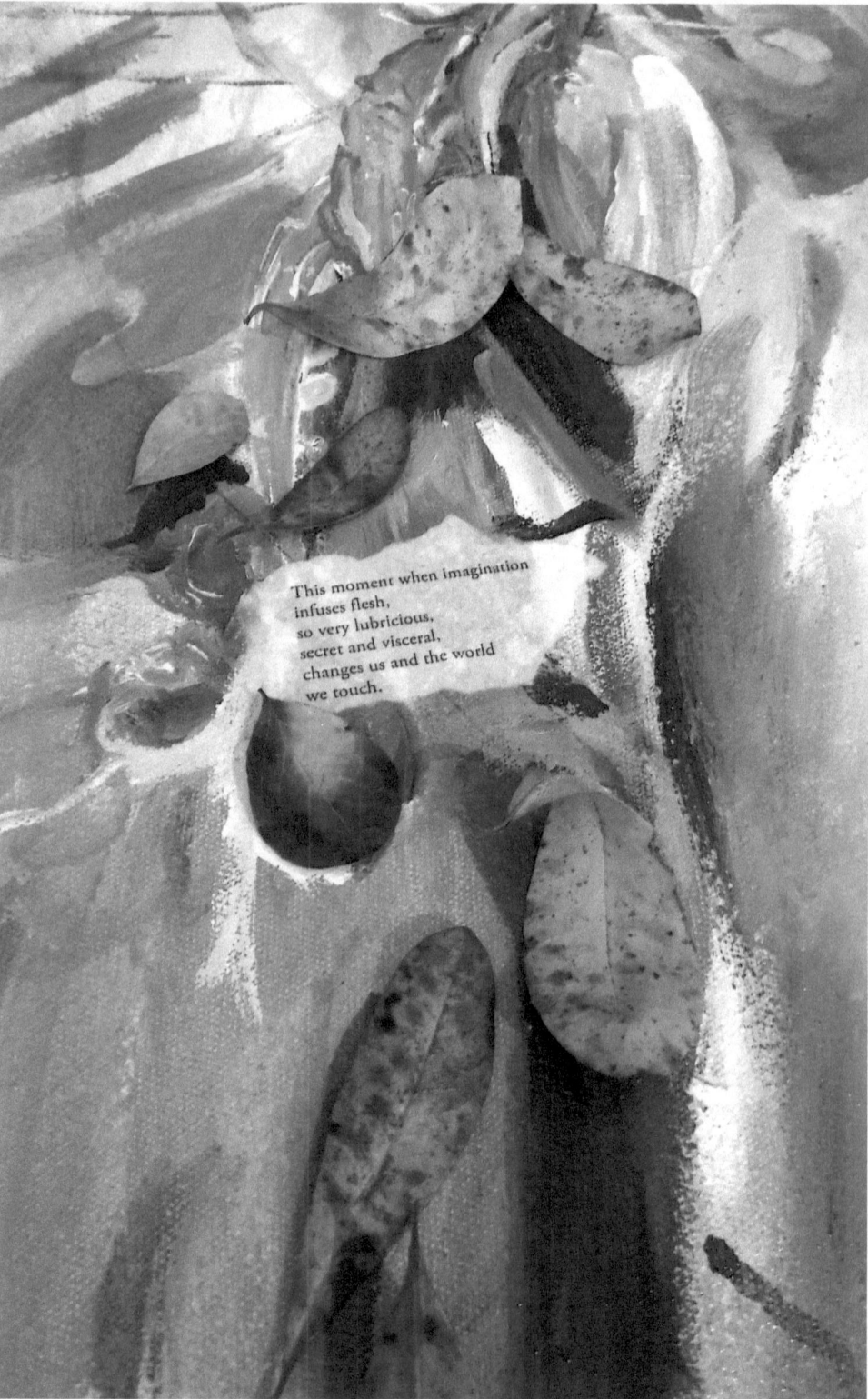

CREATING

CREATING

To wander
on our blundering, exultant way,
our only one,
from here to here
to here to here to here,
hearing
what doesn't need deciphering.
Yes, it's really come to this
simplicity.
My largest statue yet
lacks a head and hands.
They've been sitting before her
a year now, like mute
offerings.

CARRY-ONS

*The only journeys I want to take now
are inner ones*, I tell my sister
as just minutes into the new year
we circle the parking lot
of her Florida condo dragging
empty suitcases, a ritual
from her adopted country
designed to lure luck
and high adventure.

My words wing free of me
like the cries of hungry gulls.
The little wheels rumble
around us like surf,
Turning away from her appraising gaze
(she is younger and still aches
with wanderlust), I swear I hear
something rustling
with portent and impatience
inside the zippered case
I borrowed from her
without inspection.

DISMISSALS

Tsh! Tsh! Tsh! Swishh! Swishh!
Birds are seeking refuge in the trees,
humans in houses. Lawns pulse
with green carapaces. It's creepy.
Locusts are discharging seventeen years
of dreams and inchoate longings
in broad daylight, oblivious to decorum,
danger. On porches and swing sets,
back lawns and rock gardens, rooftops, fenders,
shirt collars, hat brims, and pant cuffs,
they're matching up their body parts
with those of total strangers,
making an unholy critch and crssshhh and crik
under boot heels and stilettos.

I imagine what preceded this, all those years
in which they gently fed on tree roots, as oblivious
to each other's existence as eggs in ovaries, but more
than a promise, a partial possibility, they were
complete in themselves, needing nothing but time
to come to maturity, and maybe knowing it.
I wonder what shaped itself in that long darkness
and spreads its wings now, knows itself
by sheer propulsion into light, heat, flight,
random collision, climax, collapse.

This isn't taking place anywhere around me.
Here we only have ants and some ravenous slugs
and slimy ground beetles. Here wrens swoop
to feed on raspberries, robins fluster
the standing water in the creek,
cardinals flash among the poplar leaves,
each one singing its own song, listening
keenly for its own kind. Do they ever
recognize each other? I ask my husband
and he says, That's what song is for.
But I don't mean robin to robin, cardinal
to cardinal, starling to starling, crow
to crow. Do mockingbirds hear hawks,
hummingbirds hear owls. I mean the way I hear
each of them starting before dawn.
I mean the way in my own dreams I hear
those carapaces collapsing whenever I think to leave
a solitude so deep in me it feels like destiny.

What has taken shape in that darkness,
what deep roots have served as nurture?
What wild mystery will set it free
and what is out there waiting to match it
so perfectly that it, too, has to be seen
to be believed?

IF WE WERE TO OPEN THAT KNOT

If we were to open that knot
in my gut, my love,
what would we find inside it?
A loose tooth.
A spider's web binding
a rusted razor blade.
Lips of clay, dissolving.
A hive hum.
The flicker of a goldfish's tail.
The elegant, interminable segments
of a tapeworm. A sliver
of an old woman's fingernail.
A veil.
The mud encrusted point
of an upended croquet wicket.
Damned anagrams:
devil and lived,
santa and satan,
eve.

SOURCE NOTES

Stunned, brown, no bigger
than a grandchild's palm,
it lies motionless
on the floor of the deep
stainless steel sink
while my screams soar
out windows and doors
to meld with the amazing thrum
of tree frogs, blare of sirens
racing to the hospital or jail.
My husband tenderly trusses it
in an old towel and releases it
from our front porch and it glides
toward our creek, all those
luscious mosquitoes.

But there's no end to this story
it seems. The bat, so splatted
and unconscious, still rests
against the steel, my screams
as strange to me as this comatose
creature, still swoop and soar.
There is no door. Only me, stock
still, listening to what's pouring
so involuntarily from me, looking
at what can't see back, can't act.
We don't kill them anymore,
these forlorn, loam-dark prayers
that tumble from attics into our studios,
disoriented by their own hunger
for fixed stars and fitful fireflies.

We don't kill them anymore
because there are stiff fines
for disturbing the ecosphere.
Now, we remove and exclude.
The width of a number two pencil,
one woman whispers. That's all they need.
They can sleep there, whole colonies,
for years without you suspecting anything.
I'm at the age where my mind
is a sieve. It's that fountain of sound
I want to bathe in again, how
pure and powerfully thoughtless
it was. But it just flows through.
What remains is that dark, stunned
source—just the reality of it,
so small, dense, and different,
and the heartbreaking irreconcilability
of cause and consequence.

OPEN VEINS

I take it as a sign
when the pages of my old Galeano book
threaten to fly away
from this rooftop on Calle Crespo,
where I've set it down so carefully
to savor and ponder—
over a hot cup of coffee smoothed with chocolate.
Set it down as if we had all the time in the world
to *recordar*, which Galeano writes
comes from the Latin *re-cordis*,
to return through the heart.
An observation I immediately understood
as a blessing, one that has set the pace,
the theme, for my time here.
I think he might delight in the white flurry,
and question my impulse to pull the untethered
pages back into his original order. For hasn't he,
a decade older than me, recently renounced
the most acclaimed work of his youth?
Why should I be bound to my style
of thirty-seven years ago?
It was too heavy.

His gift, he's learned, is what *not*
to say, how to let mystery
circulate freely, between images,
words, moments of exquisite
irony, pain and truth in momentary
equipoise. To understand it all returns,
exile, torture, mad love, bewilderment and
wonder.

And reconfigures.
And reconfigures.
And reconfigures.

GIRL IN THE GRIP OF AN IDEA

i
"I have an *idea*," she says, walking in circles
around the table, her eyes lifted, seeing
something we can't. A dance performance
where she stars. A selva where lionesses roam
in prides, hiding from hyenas, and she
is their fearless leader. An orchestra she conducts,
one that excludes her whimsical little sister
who gamely joins in but doesn't
play to her tempo, steals the spotlight.

She keeps rearranging the instruments,
running the scene through her mind.
"And then she will play like *this*,"
she says to herself crossly, her sticks
bouncing wildly off the small marimba.
"I won't have it," she decides and restricts
the instruments to adults. But they insist,
as they assume their drums and rattles,
and chiming glasses of water,
that she include the marimba, her eager
little sister, and its not, not, *not*
like she imagined. Light drains
from her face, the room.

In this family where genes don't define us,
where identifications cross often and unpredictably,
freely ignoring bloodlines and shared histories,
my granddaughter and I are facing off again.
But let me begin with her beauty, the way,
when alight with hope, gripped by an idea,
joy thrums through her and she leaps in place
or races in circles, her long gold hair floating free,

shouting, *Yes! Yes! Yes!*
The whole world seems to expand to receive her
and we too experience it as more capacious, illumined.

ii
But now I am standing firmly between her and her idea,
and I don't understand that she isn't responsible,
that she is in the *grip* of her idea, not the other way
around, and that she can't obey me because that grip
is stronger than us both. It leads her to light stoves,
clamber on counter tops to try to reach the basket
she needs to complete the picnic she imagines
she will take us all on as soon as it is filled.
It led her at three to lift a special red vase of mine
and, looking straight at me, eyebrows raised, smiling,
dash it to the ground. Has led her today, at six,
to lift and drop an even heavier book—
unexpectedly—on her sister's head.

Days before her grandfather, stumbling
in a darkened room as he positioned himself
to watch a lunar eclipse, shattered a tall,
heavy, clay sculpture of my making.
Gathering up the shards, the purity
of my rage astounded me. I beat the floor yelling,
"How *could* you? How *could* you?"
If I had tired of it, decided to destroy it myself,
there would have been another kind of pleasure—
but this—to come between me and my *way*
before I had completely absorbed its energy . . .
"You have no idea, no *idea*," I said.
And he, stunned with remorse, kept whispering,
like a chastened boy, "*So* sorry."

iii
She doesn't slam the floor and ask me
how *could* you stand between me and my
life current—and I don't, like my mother,
call her a horrible, horrible girl,
although I touch the scar over my right
eyebrow where my sister, similarly gripped,
aimed a metal swing. "Did you *hear* me?"
I ask her, all these energies, these loosed
identifications swirling inside me
like a hungry flock of crows.
She doesn't answer, she just stares.
Whatever is holding her at this moment
is still as quicksand, just as demanding.
A single word might swallow her.
She *can't* say she's sorry. She *can't* say
she won't do it again.

And *I* can't say I won't ask her to—
because she is a child and I am not
the grandmother she imagined.
But I *am* an artist who knows
that imagined gardens need real
toads in them if they are to become
poetry—and that little girls
if they are to dream resiliently, live
creatively, need real women,
dense, intractable, gripped
just as powerfully by their own ideas,
to block them now and then.

SYMBIOSIS

i
As we walk the cloud forest, I keep seeking
out the bromeliads growing in the crevasses
of the banyan trees, which they call here *higuerons*.
As an artist, it is not only the thing itself that fascinates,
but the metaphors it invites, supports.
They're offering bowls, these epiphytes,
shimmering with condensed cloud, fertile dust.
They can grow amazingly large on nothing
but air and the mulch from a few wayward leaves,
up there, way up there, where the branches fork
and the sun seeps. What would it feel like
just to live where you alight,
so open and so self-contained, flourishing
on sunshine, mist, wind, all you're asking
of the world around you is just this,
your presence in the midst.

Thinking so, I hear a rustle high in the canopy,
glimpse a flash of red and blue—
a quetzal—and on the path before me
a file of beautiful young women all pause
their eyes upraised, their heads tipped back,
solemn, awed, as if they were sharing a visitation
of the Virgin. That image, unsought, will feed me for days.

ii
And then there are those towering *higueron*s themselves
with their cascades of aerial roots, some thick as trees,
and the profusion of vines and ferns and mosses,
orchids and bromeliads, quetzals and bell birds
they support. I'm in love with their mass
and their hospitality and the way their buttress roots,
some as tall as me, snake out in all directions,
the way you can slip inside their hollowed cores,
arms stretched high or wide. They provide
a hundred ways to feel safe.

But their metaphors discomfit. All this from a single fig seed
sown by a wasp high up there in the canopy.
Immediately they seek the earth not sky,
their aerial roots hungrily snaking down,
gaining density, mass, as slowly
they strangle the tree that innocently hosts them.
From so little, so much, but at such unanticipated cost.

It makes me think about how a story
can begin with just the smallest germ of an idea—
and then an image or a character moves in
with a vitality all its own and gradually takes over
and you're both excited and appalled because it isn't under
your conscious control at all and yet something bigger
and more intriguing and filled with life is coming into being,
something in which you can shelter, consoled and amazed,
relieved and also chastened, wondering why we ever
try to put our names to something we ultimately
had so little hand in making.

FIGMENT

I want to be a figment
of imagination, my own
imagination. An aspiration.
I can see her in the distance,
just there where sleep merges
with Rumi's mystical open.
The wind whispers so
intimately in my own ear,
I shiver as I watch her
breast-stroking through grasses
higher than she. They just seem
to move like the sea. In reality
they are knife sharp and her skin
is no thicker than mine. But she's
smiling, imagining how she will feel
when she reaches me and I pull her to me,
my touch as primordial and as healing
as yearning that knows itself returned.

THIS MOMENT

This moment when imagination
infuses flesh,
so very lubricious,
secret and visceral,
changes us and the world
we touch.

This place,
so very lubricious, secret and visceral,
where imagination infuses flesh
is quiet, inextricably personal
and vast, and capable of holding
equitably, just imagine,
equitably—
brushfire and mist,
listlessness and flights of pure
pleasure, solar eclipses,
moonrise, an infant's first laugh,
the word we can't take back,
opossum, robin, and white tiger,
first sap, fish thrash, skidding
clouds, doubt, surmise,
and the way your eyes after long absence
travel so slowly over the whole of me—

This place, so very lubricious,
secret, and visceral, is capable of holding
every one of them equitably,
just imagine, *equitably,*
until we know them all
as well as we know ourselves.

Which is little,
blessedly little.

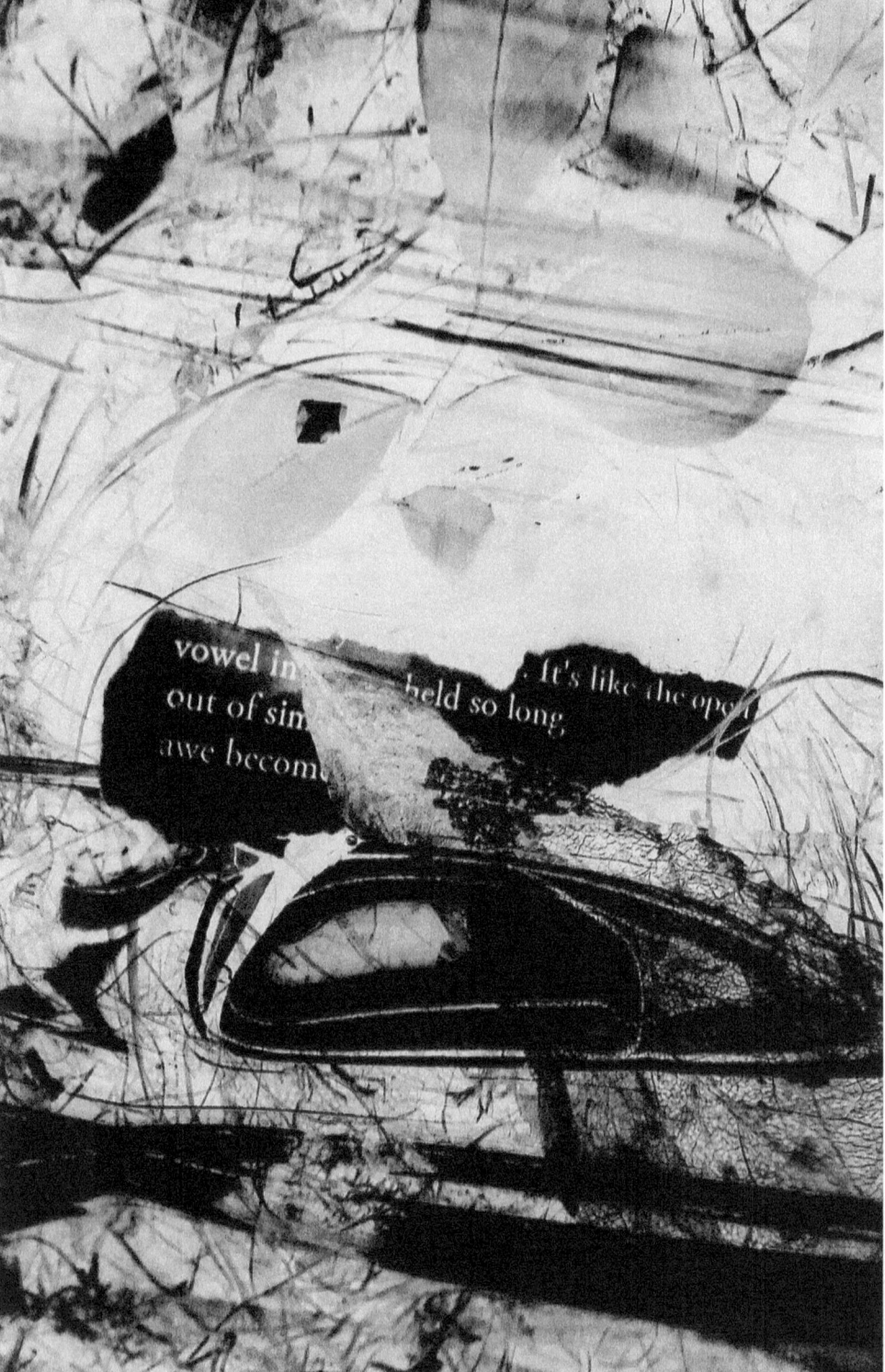

THE SECRET SWEETNESS OF VEJEZ

WHO SAYS?

Who says water that reaches
the sea has forgotten
its source? Or sweat
that hides now in cumulus
clouds has forgotten my brow?
Who says freedom doesn't have death
as its final destination?
Who says age can't be luxurious,
astonishing, *sui generis*?

THE SECRET SWEETNESS OF VEJEZ

is the way we feel when strange beds
fit themselves to us rather than we to them,
the way we no longer need to translate
the slight hesitation, the sideways glance,
the swallowed sigh or closed eyes—
or shut off the yelp of delight
that rises when we turn the corner
and find the ocean expanding in a pure blue
circle around us as if we are
the axis mundi.

CAROLINA SUMMER

Why should a casual August outing
with her sister and brother to pick blackberries
in one of her father's fields
open such a floodgate to mourning?
Was it really sixty years ago?
She doesn't see herself as old,
but she, the firstborn, still lives
and breathes—while they are savoring
before their parents, before her,
a sweetness that stains their hands
and mouths like blood. They are sharing
the ripe wild fruit of eternity, while she
feels bitterly alone as if she,
the most obedient of them,
the most dutiful, the most devout,
has been permanently denied
some essential favor.

I SAW THE LINES

I saw the lines
inside my curved hand
and something magical happened.
My own tree of life
branching.

I JUST WANT TO LIE UP HERE IN THE DARK

I just want to lie up here in the dark
listening to the doves, discovering
something I never suspected
about love. Breakdown or
breakthrough, there's much
to be said for and against
a name. When I came here
a wiser voice than mine inside
me said, *You must begin to believe
in death as a completion,
a homecoming,
if you are ever to be at rest
inside your own skin.*

It's true. I'm tired of living
defended, but I can't will belief.
I can let it seep into me today
the way tears seep out, unannounced,
the way slow rain, the gracious sound of it,
seeps into my consciousness as still
and welcoming and gray as midday.

Sun on my feet, rain clouds moving to the east,
the long dripping leaves lilt gently
in a light wind, distant mariachi trumpets
and wood saws and these words,
clean and piercing as a squeaking wheel,
enter and stay there like the answer to a prayer:
Be. Leave. *Believe.* Be. Leave. *Believe.*
This is the beginning of true healing.

FLOWERS ON THE SAND

i
I'm sitting here on the beach expanding
into the empty space around me, the sound
of the surging sea, the constant reconfigurations
of bathers, pelicans, foaming waves, lazy clouds,
catamarans, and surfers clutching their boards,
always poised to catch the next,
the next, the next overwhelming swell.

It feels like the first time in weeks you've been
out of sensing distance. It's become our habit
when we travel out here in the bright, wide world,
this shoulder to shoulder stance, the exchanged glance
that lets us know we've shared focus, intrigue, delight.
The proximity is like a hand pausing a millimeter away
from the hairs on the skin. It heightens everything.

But this morning, I wanted a moment all to myself,
so I could hold and be held by the wonder of our tropical
winter, like an intimate and open secret—
like our completeness now in ourselves and
in each other. I would never have guessed
in my mid-forties that this is where my life led.
Never. Ever. I was fully set, I believed,
in the opposite, isolate, direction.

ii
Small yellow trumpet flowers, once part
of a large cluster pulsing high in the leafless
Guayacán tree, now tumble past one by one.
Each is so perfect in itself, you'd never know
they were ever part of something larger.
Each one follows the impulse of its own liberating gust,
establishing its own unique trajectory, waking me
to the subtle, unpredictable variations
in this seemingly steady wind.

Suddenly I think of my close friends
who have been married far longer than we,
deeply, contentedly so, whose husbands now
are slowly failing from Parkinson's, dementia.
How all the losses are like these flowers,
each so small and gold and complete in itself,
astonishingly beautiful, irreversible, whole.

The winds shift, the blossoms with their open
throats tumble nearer, farther, nearer. My eyes tear
and my own throat closes: There's nothing I can say
to my dear friends except what I hope they will say to me,
or you, should it become necessary:
We have all been so graced with happiness.

I have to believe that out of this joy-steeped grief—
received—another kind of fullness, however erratic
and windblown, will come.

IF I COULD CHOOSE

If I could choose
the sweep of your love
it would touch eternity.

If I could choose its width
it would fit inside me.
If I could choose its sweetness
it would cling to the tongue
like honey and lemon.

It would be solid as sand
and hot as coals
and free as the sea
to lift me, lift me
and hold me close.

If I could choose
the length of your love
I would be conceived inside it
and ride it like a rising breath
through life, through death,
a sound, a song, a home
where we are one.

If I could choose.

THE WIND IS HAVING ITS WAY TODAY

The wind is having its way today
with the palms and the myrtles.
They're waving, whipping, kowtowing
right and left. The clouds above
are snow white and motionless.
We're outdoing ourselves with small,
thoughtful gestures—dark chocolate
with chili, straw fedoras, lilies, drop cloths
and maps, fresh bread, tulips—knowing them all
as we hand them happily back and forth
to be totally unnecessary. It's like the open
vowel in a song held so long
out of simple delight
awe becomes part of it.

THE COLOR OF HONEY

There is a sweetness hidden in me
the color of honey deep in a sealed womb,
indistinguishable from muscle, blood,
the troubling loss of lust. It can't be
reached, breached. It can't be seen
to be believed, and yet I do
believe I do and don't owe
its existence to you, the way your hands
held out, held on through those long
years of primal sorrow, how they waked
and slaked something even deeper
than bereft, some indestructible yes
that gave meaning to all the rest.

Every night, to help you sleep,
you eagerly pull me to you as if
my mere existence, just flesh stretched
over a dark so complete that within it
color and all it signifies are nothing,
as if just this, truly, were the fullness of life.
You're no longer asking for more.
It's another kind of grief, what I feel
at the resignation I imagine
flows so steadily through you.

Sealed tight, the two of us. Still thrumming.
It's not right—and it's right
not to fight it. There is a sweetness
in me that weeps to be known
as inextinguishable—and freely given.
I hear it clearly as you breath slows and deepens.
In my eyes, it must be seen to be believed,
but every night you teach me differently.

TRUST THE EMPTINESS WITHIN

Trust the emptiness within
and the rain sifting gently
through palm, jacaranda and mimosa.
Church bells tolling for joy,
east and west, north and south,
on *el Día de la independencia*,
For we never begin again. We beget.
And forget.

And beget again
watching hummingbirds hover,
then rest, wings closed
on the smallest twig
on the one dead branch
of the largest, most vibrant tree
in our borrowed garden.

The doves above take without stint
what the world freely gives,
leaf cover, air to breathe and spread
their wings in, yet one more
moment of perfect tranquility
fully absorbed into our being
like manna received for what it really is.

We are not here to be saved, redeemed,
transformed. We are just here to live.
Even the dove turns its back on us.
The hummingbird moves to its own
inner *ritmo,* and out on the street,
a world away, a minute, cars
and trucks slur through the residue
of a hurricane to the east of us,
a typhoon to the west.

We're drenched in goodness.
Fíjese. Just *fíjese.*
At our age. Let's stay this way
as long as the hummingbird,
and the dove and the light above.

*LETTERS TO MY SON,
TWENTY YEARS A MAN*

ÓRALE, HIJO MÍO

Órale, hijo mío, la mujer que cantaba
con la voz de un ángel lloraba
al mismo tiempo con una intensidad
tan quieta, tan completa
que su oración entró en mi corazón
y la llevé conmigo afuera de la iglesia,
la llevé adentro de mi propria vida
como luz insólita, pura necesidad.
Vendería mi alma—al diablo o a dios,
si creyera—por una voz como la suya,
una voz que sabe que nuestro último consuelo
vive adentro de nuestros dolores
más inagotables.

LISTEN, MY SON

Listen, my son, the woman who sang
with the voice of an angel cried
at the same time with an intensity
so still, so complete
that her prayer entered my heart
and I carried it with me outside the church,
took it inside my own life,
a rare light, pure necessity.
I would sell my soul—to the devil or god,
if I believed—for a voice like hers,
a voice that knows our ultimate consolation
lives inside our most inexhaustible pains.

NO CALL, NO CARD

Ni una llamada. Ni una carta.
When I pause, I hear the minutes ticking,
telling more than time. You are always
on my mind. Two minutes,
how hard could that be? The ire rises,
tried, true, and tired. You will never
need the assurance of my breath the way
I need yours. No words. Like a new mother
blocking the hall light as she stands
at the nursery door, listening, just listening
until she can hear her own heartbeat
steadied by the delicate rasp
that tells her as nothing else can
that life is not too much
for either of them. When I give up
trying to reach you and just listen in,
this silence between us has that same rasp.
I let it steady me. If you were to call
and tell me what I most fear—that you are heartsick,
hopeless really, at sixty-two and forty, honestly
what could I do to relieve it?

This morning I hear doves, cars rumbling
over cobblestones, the scratching of my pen,
my husband in the next room, stirring.
I try to hold them all, imperturbably, steadily,
with breathing room between.
I am practicing—for you.

PALOMAS

The mourning doves are tumbling
from the trees scattering small cries
of surprise. Sounds that, eyes closed,
could be mistaken for those of startled
babies, although the fierce, rising
fluster of wings belies this.

On the other side of the tiled wall
a boy of ten I've never seen
bellows with a man's authority
every evening from six to eight.
I've been told he is autistic
and believes he is the lead
singer in a rock band. What I hear
is the purest self-assurance and glee.
Some days his younger brother sings
in solidarity, the rawest of harmonies.
No one ever complains.

It makes me grieve for all the security
I never knew to give you.
It consoles me too. Here, on the balcony,
both of us a million miles and several decades away
from the terrors I once put us through
for love, *pinche, putamadre* love.

LETTERS TO MY SON, TWENTY YEARS A MAN

i
Here in this tranquil garden—where leaves barely
quaver, white sheets hang slack as becalmed sails
on every rooftop, and birds busily crunch
their songs like seeds—I'm relieved
by dream and haunted by memory.
So, I begin with what I know to be the light
at the end of a long tunnel of *culpabilidad*
that I still hesitate to enter, it feels so deep,
so dark, so horrendous to the touch.

This morning, as a young man chimed his knife
against a metal lid and old women lugged
their trash to the curb, I woke from a dream
so simple and straightforward even I
could see and accept the gift of it.
In it, we are not alone, you and I, there is
a third party, mine, who relieves the intensity.
We're out in the open, on a bridge.
We're talking about maps of Brooklyn, the kind
you make in your mind all the time, food maps,
monument maps, sites of lost causes, but this one
you've committed to paper. "It's in our truck," you say
leading us down the ridge to a large red one.
You're referring, with that "our", to your wife,
your married life. "Actually," you say with a laugh,
tapping its door, "it's not ours, it's mine."

I'm relieved you have claimed something for yourself.
The workman's boots you wear have metal toes.
On the truck bed, glinting in the sun, well-used
tool chests, pneumatic drills, sledge hammers.
I woke wondering why it has taken me so long
to recognize your competence and manhood
when it is so obvious, and obviously such
a relief to both of us.

ii
In Atotonilco last Sunday we stepped down
from the bus and were immediately swept up
in a stream of pilgrims, women old
and young, all dressed in their indigenous
best, immaculate pinafores over bright
skirts and blouses, their heads shaded
by lace mantillas or faded rebozos,
all of them singing the same refrain,
Somos las ovejas perdidas, sálvanos o Señor.

As if I were unquestionably one
of them, they touched my hands, lifted me
with the raw force of their voices,
the stellar chiming of hundreds of small bells,
and we coursed together down the narrowing alley
toward the church's back door. Scandalized,
a male proctor pulled me aside and redirected me
toward the public entrance. Already blessed,
smilingly I acquiesced.

We met them again on the other side, now busy buying
recycled bottles filled with holy water, eyeing
bright plastic pails and baskets from China, fingering
over-priced rosaries, beribboned cloth dolls with stitched
vacuous smiles, and long, colorful, coarse jute ropes.
They settled down in doorways and on stone curbs
to review their purchases, share their tortillas, coke.

I have a bad feeling, I confided to my husband,
as I looked at their beautiful, smiling faces—
and at those ropes in purple, hot pink, green and blue
that criss-crossed their breasts like ammunition belts.
They have to be decorative, he said. But when questioned,
the chubby boy at the tienda animatedly showed us
exactly how to use the lashes that sold for half the price
of rosaries, a third the price of bells.

Pero, en realidad, no se usan, I protested. They don't really—
Sí, sí, señora, his mother assured me. *En los retiros
todas las usan. Sí, es muy commún aquí. Se llaman disciplinas.*
They're sold in pairs, the long and short of sin and expiation.
To remember the day, I chose my own pair, purple—
and a book of *alabanzas,* praises, to sing.

My son, I wish you could have seen how they took me,
so much taller, so much whiter, unquestioningly in,
as if there were something numinous in me too.
Something that isn't in my face when I stare
at those brightly dyed *disciplinas*
that feel sacrilegious to discard, shameful
to keep—or when I think of the distances
between us.

iii
Last night I woke, *asustada,* from deep sleep.
What if, in this long silence between us
that I am teaching myself to trust as healing,
creative, I miss some crucial warning sign,
take as celebratory the last wave of a drowning man?
I wrote to you immediately: *I need to hear your voice.*

I called you this morning and it was true,
just the timbre of your voice was all the assurance
needed. Even after all these years apart, I refuse
to imagine the world without you.

It was enough to share the most innocuous
of observations, how in our comings and goings here
we're always greeted by a small dog with stunted tail,
who, penned away by herself her first year,
never learned to bark. She's won my heart
and I wonder how someone who is fed so deeply
by intonations can be so attached
to her silence too.

You don't have to explain anything, I said.
Just promise me if your way gets too dark, too isolated,
you will call on us. Of course, you said, in that kind,
attentive, completely credible way you have
that, true or false, never fails to calm.

It's enough, for now, to go on.
I often gave you less.

iv
Two images keep coming back to me from that year
when you were fifteen and I was three years
younger than you are now. I'd brutally uprooted us
yet again for a man, one who had by then left us,
alone, speechless, in a country more foreign by the day.
You towered over the Mexicans streaming down
the streets of the D.F. into the metro. Your height
was the only thing that kept you from total
panic most of the time: however buffeted,
you still could see over the crowns of their heads.

But that evening on the metro as we entered
the car, we were separated by the pressure
of the people pushing behind us. I was lifted
off my own feet. The doors closed. You were
visible but beyond my reach. I could see
the beads of sweat forming on your pale freckled skin.
Mom, you said. The world is going black on me.
Relax, I said, terrified. You can't fall.

When the doors opened, I pushed ruthlessly
against the human tsunami screaming,
Mi hijo, mi hijo. Dragging you from the train,
supporting you, a foot taller, as you rocked,
silent, wretched, blind—and still unreasonably
trusting. What other alternative, really,
had I given you?

v
The man I'd upended our world for
had a bad habit when enraged
of abandoning me in the middle of the night
in distant parts of that difficult, dangerous city,
insisting, since I was so damned independent
and American, I could find my own way home.
Stranded, I would call you and, voice breaking,
assure you I would be back soon.

When I think about it now, decades
later, in this quiet, extravagant garden,
in this small, cultured town filled
with privileged Americans who have retired
at least for a time, from their families,
their past lives, as well as their *país,*
I feel something far keener than guilt.

I feel just what that must have been like for you,
those hours you waited, never knowing
if I was alive or dead, worthy of rage or respect,
wondering who you could turn to if, this time,
I betrayed the one promise you couldn't live without.

vi
I don't know what to do with this wash of time.
Hummingbirds swoop feverishly in and out
of the bougainvillea. White butterflies hover
over long purple blooms of salvia,
palomas pair off in the jacaranda.
Your own wife may be leaving you,
or may not be, she's not talking—
and you, either way, are holding
the door open for her.

I have nothing, absolutely nothing
to say to guide you. I would give anything
to know what you learned from me back then
that can help you now, although I imagine
the real question is what I can learn from you,
both then and now, that lets me see you,
you alone, as the truly free
shaper of your own destiny.

LOS VOLADORES

Their axis mundi was askew.
They knew. We all did.
The list was hard to miss. Silently,
the brightly costumed men eyed
the spiked iron fence toward which
the tall pole ominously tilted. Balloon sellers,
mariachis, families leaving the *parroquia*
in their Sunday best eddied around them
as silently they poked and loosened flagstones
with small sticks, prodded, restacked a few,
then walked away, stared skyward,
earthward, eyes wide, faces grave.

Murmuring softly, they shrugged, donned
headdresses, cradled drums, and began
to call the crowds in. Silently, hand over hand,
four of them clambered up the pole using
large yellow ropes knotted to a spinning
mandala at the top. As their leader held out
his plumed helmet seeking donations,
I couldn't keep from asking, and he
immediately agreed, *Sí, sí, no es estable.
Es peligroso. Muy peligroso.
Pero nada va a pasar, gracias a Dios.*

No one else looked the way I felt.
Compromised. Was it my duty to stop them,
not to keep looking so haplessly on and up
to where four men in fetal curves, now bound
round with ropes, waited for the pole to stop
shuddering in the windless twilight?
I told you about this, not at such length,

of course, and with feeling deleted, just
shared the photo of the four men
huddled together up there like recalcitrant fledglings.

Were they thinking about their wives, their children?
Something important they still wanted to do?
Were they remembering how many times before
they had successfully pitched themselves, in unison,
head first, earthward? I am absolutely sure
not a damn one of them thought about his mother.
In their shoes, I wouldn't either. But in mine,
I have to say, I thought of you as I leaned
myself to right and left, trying to keep that
axis mundi aligned with the space between
my own eyes. This isn't a cautionary tale
about the limited power of magical thinking.
It's just about *así es*. I couldn't help myself
anymore than they could.

In time the pole stopped quivering.
The fifth man clambered up. The four
voladores threw themselves, spread-eagled,
to their fate, spinning down down down
through the twilight, the rising sea
of sighs, while the fifth, motionless,
steadied their descent. I caught that part,
the pure euphoria of it, in real time,
hoping as I did so to share it with you
somewhere, someday.

DÉCIMAS FOR MY SON IN HIS FIFTH DECADE

i
I'm announcing the death of solipsism.
Making a funeral notice, pasting
it on lamp posts, peeling walls, not wasting
a chance—here in this underpass! The rhythm
modulates anger, doesn't purge. The schism
has always been there. Someone's watching you
lose yourself in the mirror, but what do
you see reflected in your own eyes? Lies
or deep truths, ennui or reprieve? Wise
up, look out. Someone's hurting. *It's not you.*

ii
Seriously, it's not all about you.
You never asked for your own existence,
for your fair skin, green eyes, pure resistance
to cruelty in the abstract, no clue
to the damage paralysis would do.
You turned blue at two rather than hit back.
Now you claim the power behind this act,
but the one attacking is siamese
twin to the one receiving the blow. Tease
them apart and your very heart would crack.

iii
I see it clearly now when I look back—
how this freezing has shaped you, the excuses
I've made to evade that truth. The world chooses
for you, guts dreams, drops others in your lap.
What if it isn't a choice, you really can't act—
and grace refuses to step in again?
What then? What then? What then? *What then?*
Potential has a shelf life. Your despair
chills us here in Cartagena. We dare
not tell you what it does to us—*again.*

iv
Forty-four years, *real* promise. I have been
its faithful, berated keeper. But now
I'm as tired as you of the cost. How
do we give up without giving in
to the despair it shields us both from? *Then*
what? So many paths, now closed, you refused
to see when open to you. What gets loosed
now, when your eyes are open but your way
is not? What opens, closes on that day
when *I* pull out? Will you feel soothed? Misused?

CALL WAITING

Loving mothers hold out futures
for their children, so many
open doors. They take what they know
about us and keep blowing it up
into a vision they expect us to fulfill.
At what point does that innocent
hope and cherishing faith distort,
diminish, and condemn us
to failures not of our own making?
When do we refuse to assume
that yoke of disappointment
and with it all the good
intentions that built it?

When do mothers become equally
intransigent? When do we refuse
to be an excuse, or even
an explanation? I am breathless
with excess fluid they have pumped
into me after removing my uterus
and ovaries. Honestly, I wasn't sure
you would call to check on me
after surgery—a lapse I understood
would be driven by anxiety more
than indifference. But you did.
Three days later, just returned from hours
at the emergency room, the onset
of congestive heart failure, you call again,
but even when told, seem oblivious,
acting as if, as always, I am only there to hear.
I can't get my words out. My heart
can't take the weight of this third spacing.
I hang up.

You are years older now than I was
when I last made any decision for you.
What weighs on you most are the expanding
implications of your own choices. How long
has it taken me to stop reducing your life
to my own mistakes? How long will it take you
to do the same? Where does it begin?

The phone rings and rings. The sound
keeps expanding around me. I trust you
to keep calling.

MONTEVERDE

It feels like the home of a man who has outlived
any need to keep secrets from himself—
all windows and skylights and warm wood
and vistas. Clouds constantly condense, dissolve
along the summit. It's hypnotic. Healing.
We're here for three days, but it feels
as if we're here to stay, with the wind
whipping the banana leaves and pines,
the agoutis nosing up and down the drive
setting the three dogs next door into eerily
harmonious cacophony that birds punctuate
with long piercing cries.

Our first night, I wake to the irregular pulse
of the endless wind, my mind racing,
my stomach a dense dark stone of dread
heavy enough to drown me. I was dreaming
about my son and a woman he met while he was waiting
in line with me. I was returning something.
Entranced, the two of them couldn't stop talking,
or take their eyes off each other. While I,
entangled in some ludicrous bureaucratic mobius strip,
was missing one essential number on my receipt
so needed to repeat the whole process infinitely.
There was a turnstile I had to keep returning to.
Each time I would look over at the two of them,
but they never looked up, they were so lost
in each other, and I was relieved to see my son
beginning to ease the deep isolation of his last few years.

But then as dreams do, the scene shifted without warning,
and my son was calling me on the phone to tell me
frankly about years of drinking he had until now
concealed from me, much worse than the worst
I had ever imagined, bringing all the growth
and assertion and confidence of the last few years
into question. He was telling me long after the fact,
but I was still listening in present tense, wondering what
else he had been and was still holding back. I couldn't bear
to let go of the hope he had been building in me—
or of the fear it wouldn't hold.

I wake breathless, dizzy, and you hold me.
The dream still feels unspeakable,
but my responses to it—my racing heart, aching gut,
the electric charge of these night terrors—do not.
You respond to those as if they are all part
of a normal cloud forest night
with its forceful, pulsing wind, leaves rattling
on the orange trees, the drip of water
from the cooling roof, ping plop, ping plop,
intrusive and mundane as a leaking faucet.

I lie here after your breath has slipped back
into the slower oscillations of sleep,
grateful for your touch, for the warmth
of these blankets and comforter, the warmth
of the wood walls in this simple, numinous
house. I think about the taxi driver
who drove us back from the grocery store
in his red pick-up, turning right, left,
as we told him to, then pausing a second,
silent, when he pulled up to the cabin.
"I built this house. I built it with my older brother.
I did not always drive a taxi. I built things."

He looked back at us, shaking his head.
"The owner was very old. I suppose that is why—"
We exclaimed about the exquisite woodwork, spacious
simplicity, the light. Here in the warmth
of your embrace, my own body finally quieting,
I can still see his expression, how pride was confounded
by something more intricate, difficult, perhaps something
about his brother, some place where pain and pleasure
were still inextricably bound.

I think as well about the stories
I'm making now without knowing it—
the ones that rise up unbidden in the night,
as if strangers have just directed me
to a house I myself constructed years ago.
Like this dream that undercuts all
the warmth and trust with which my son shared
the struggles and triumphs of his last two years,
and the sweet sweet hope with which I received
what he was freely giving me.

Or this other story I don't share with anyone
about how the mental shifts of age
I'm experiencing are not normal,
rather part of a more tragic, inevitable, unspeakable story,
one that stretches back generations, mother
to mother to mother. I lie here in this house built
for a man too old to have any more secrets
from himself and ask myself *why?* —
Why *these* stories? I begin to listen.

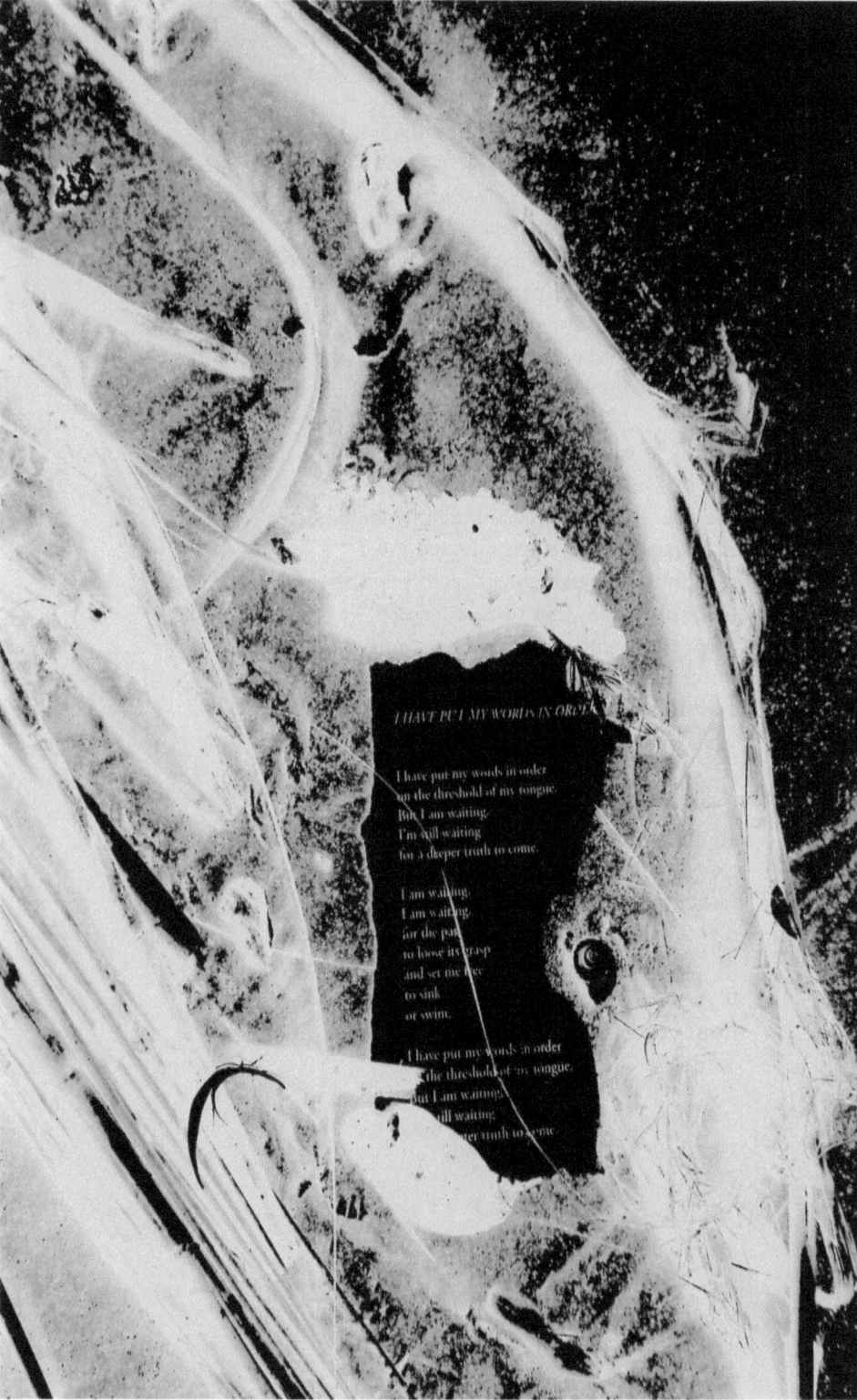

SHAKEN BABY, FOREVER HELD

WHEN THE LIGHT WAS WANING

A month ago, when the light
was waning and I was pushing so hard
toward a goal that did not feed my soul,
I would find myself suddenly sliding, tear-slaked,
down the kitchen cabinets to the floor
and I remembered, because I was nearly
there again, those terrible years
at the beginning of our wonderful marriage
and I couldn't help wondering
how you ever held in there.
For me in some ways it was simpler
because it was inescapable
and the alternative was extinction.
I remember our first year, that night
near my birthday when I found myself kneeling
in the closet in a house I didn't want to live in, just
keening and keening and keening
and I heard someone I had never met before,
a woman, an emanation, coming up behind me
and saying so clearly,
We must comfort the one who is suffering.
And I thought, listening to those sobs,
Oh, the one who is suffering is me.

WHERE STORY BEGINS

Does it always come, our public speech,
from protest and the need, the raw need
to be met? The infant crying in her crib.
The two year old, defiant, chanting,
No, No, No. Insisting she knows
her intentions better than anyone else
and she has been, God forbid, misunderstood.
Listen to how it's expressed first, this need
for redress and understanding: in the third person.
We use our first names—Heather, Nora, Ellis,
Zoë, Tor, Carrie, Kate, Cameron, Alex, Fred.
Carrie want cookie. Zoë want Tor go.
Heather need door open. Open, please.

Listen to how it expresses itself in story.
We're all flawed heroes driven to voice
and action because some expectation,
some sweet, some deep, some necessary
expectation has not been met.
The door is closed. The heart is more so.
The wild world beckons and someone
or something is standing between us
and what we must have, must reach,
must meet. And in that explanation
that story, we divorce ourselves.
We become a name, a character, later
a pronoun: *I*

I HAVE PUT MY WORDS IN ORDER

I have put my words in order
on the threshold of my tongue.
But I am waiting,
I'm still waiting
for a deeper truth to come.

I am waiting,
I am waiting,
for the past
to loose its grasp
and set me free
to sink
or swim.

I have put my words in order
on the threshold of my tongue.
But I am waiting,
I'm still waiting
for a sweeter truth to come.

THAT'S WHAT I WANT

That's what I want
with my all in all,
I want it all taken back
and my freedoms restored.

THAT'S WHAT I WANT

...ha... ...at I want
w... ...l in al...
...ll tak... ...ack
...reedoms restored,

DIALOGICS

You never heard, you never heard, you never heard

                                          A word I said.

You bet.

                                          You bettered.

Bitterly. Or so it seemed.

                          What *was* I, with such certainty, seeing?

The past's a blank, beyond retrieving. We both know

                                    I would do it all differently

This time around. But you,

                              my love, are in the ground.

Listening.

WORDS THAT NEVER KNOW AIR

I want to explore
in a way that's pure
these words that never know air
before paper. Precious. Salvific.
Secret.

Because they come to me
this way—through mute muscle—
they can never be suborned
by my craven desire to please
the other listener in me—
the one who is always looking out there
for danger, disagreement, dominance, denial.

Without meaning to, I've penned
my soul, severed her fire
and fury, her sensuous
wisdom and her power to heal
and anneal the deepest rift in me
from the material world, which she
needs as deeply as I need her.

In the years to come when the only real
challenges are the absolute ones,
illness, death, why do I persist
in this hedge against radiance?

DANGERS OF PUBLIC SPEAKING

The child, two and speechless,
blocks her mother's view
of her newborn brother's crib.
Her grief has no beginning
and no end, is pure
electricity, the skin alive
with wildfire.
Sound threatens to envelop her,
put her fire, so unbearable
and necessary, out.
Fire and water, then,
blessedly condense.
She tastes the word
as it shapes inside her,
releases it slowly,
as if she were blowing a glass globe
with her whole self, light to light
from the inside out.

*

Her next never gets said.
Her mother is on her, covers
the girl's ears with her hands
and lifts her straight from the ground
and shakes and shakes
that blameless skull
and what is inside it
senseless. Not a word,
pure vengeance that sings
a lifetime later inside
the same, quieted, mind.

*

The will and guilt of the next breath.
There are no words for that.
Or the potential, that rises,
whenever she stands before a group,
blocking from herself the reality
of death's door, and the ineradicable
knowledge of what can release it,
and exactly what can be released,
that force that lifts us without
warning out of ourselves
and shakes us senseless.
True words. Heard.

*

There is no protection, never was.
Applause stings like napalm.
Something cold and clammy, her back,
what she's up against,
what she's holding in.
True language, she understands,
only comes through
our hands. She caresses
the page.

JUST BECAUSE

Just because
the little girl
with a snarled curl
in the middle
of her muddied forehead
never said sorry
for being enchanted
by the irresistible glories
of tar, its luminous
blackness spread
like a night sky
under her bare feet, and she
discovering in that gleaming
moon-round reflection
her welcoming twin,
beaming—
just because she couldn't
stop smiling at the memory
did not make her
horrible, *horrible* girl.

Oh, I love her so, how
she looks out of the photo
sitting, grinning, on the hood
of the 50s car, smiling
just because the wind
sings and the sun touches
her skin soft as the fingertips
of the woman who crooned to her
daily, my baby, my beautiful
baby girl with the pretty curls.

Now my own face reflects back that smile
just because she's so wonderfully
stubborn and still believes,
all evidence to the contrary,
that something, someone, somewhere
wants her terribly, fiercely, fully,
exactly, just exactly, as she is.

I will rock you, rock you, rock you, I will rock you, yes I will.
I will love you, love you, love you, I will love you, yes I will.
For you're my lovely, lovely, lovely, You're my lovely, little girl.

RUSSIAN DOLLS

i
My spine is a live wire,
pure fire, phosphorus white,
burning from infancy straight
into this very night
in my seventh decade.
It is as radiant as God's mind
and it is all mine.
What I received
as my own mother's
psychotically postpartum
blessing, reactivated by age
and illness, so similar
to the one her own mother
gave her. And still I wonder
what possessed her to take
this unintelligible girl of two
and shake her beyond her wild,
remorseless mourning into a calm
only mystics should know
and return her, agnostic,
to a pain to which only saints
aspire. What sense, even now,
do I make of what I
so stubbornly held onto,
what would not, could not
let me go? Even now, graying,
my memory for proper names
porous, alone in the dark,
sleepless with this unspeakable
radiance at my core, I hear that
small child rehearsing a stance
that is still mine.

Heather hurting.
Horrible. Horrible girl.
Heather hurting.
Don't hurt Heather.
Heather hurting.
Help Heather.
Heather helping.
Don't hurt Heather.
Heather helping.
*Heather **helping.***

ii
What possesses me so I can't—or won't—
listen to the brutal senselessness
of where it all began. Chemicals surging
after a brother's birth, a tiny girl loudly
mourning a lost nanny, the accusing words
of another mother, my grandmother,
wild for a son dead days after birth,
to you, his surviving twin: *You were so greedy*
in the womb you starved your baby brother.
And there she is, my mother, obediently feeding
her own baby boy and she sees herself
in me, through her own mother's eyes—
and tries to finish what her mother
wanted to but never dared.

Why was I given to her
as a living prayer she could not,
would not hear? Why do I,
this fire searing me from within,
continue to see myself as cause,
not effect? If I hadn't been,
she wouldn't have—
Why don't I hear, instead, what that child
still living in me is still saying
to the only one still alive to respond:
Heather hurting. Help her.

iii
I imagine being left, in dementia,
with just this pain, no beginning
or end, my identity entire,
and it feels as godless and lawless
as my life at two. I imagine you, now,
remembering what you could never
openly admit to while alive,
imagine you for the first time feeling
its full effect, feeling as incandescent a pain,
as sacred a grief as I do. I imagine you
depending on me to undo it,
generation by generation,
and I imagine choosing,
once and for all, not to.
So we can both know
we really do have choices
and I was and still am
one of them. *Heather
hurting. Don't— Heather **helping.**
Heather **helping.** Help her.*

And that's what I do, imagining
it is your deepest prayer too.

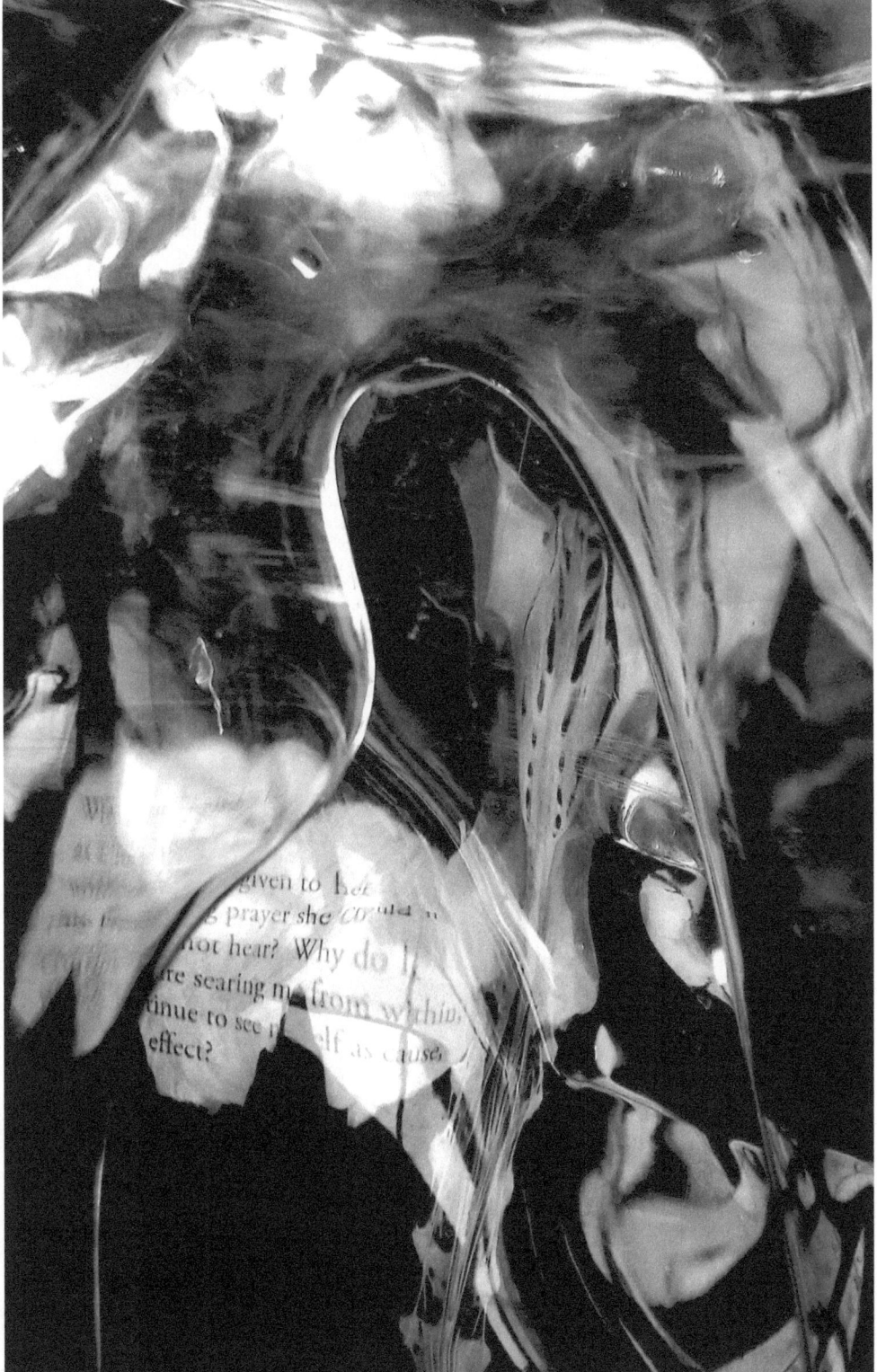

MIRROR NEURONS

It is a terrible thing to admit
that my body knows, neurons and muscles
and voice, what my mother felt
when I was two or three and she
was kicking me in a paroxysm
of pure rage. *It made her happy.*
How can I ever forgive myself
for harboring this truth just as clearly,
just as alive in my own physiology,
as how it felt to be on the receiving end?

For years now I've been listening
to the stories of men and women who did worse,
much worse, but usually not to kin.
This truth, the physical pleasure they felt provoking
fear, exercising force, never gets out
in words, but there's a humor there,
a generosity of acceptance for that younger
vainglorious and brutal self, the one a woman
defined as *having heart, and mean
and hurt and brazen.*

I've been listening and resisting,
the same way I resist the image
of our president shoving
his suffocating tongue
into the mouth of a woman trapped
alone with him in an elevator
because when I was seven
a man dressed in priestly robes
did the same thing with his penis
in my small mouth. It took forty years

to bear to hear the words he said, *Jesus
Christ, Jesus Christ*, and admit
that to me they were as filthy and as silencing
as his ejaculate.

I've never had any doubt once I could bear
to remember, that he never experienced
a minute of remorse or even remembered it,
that existential explosion in me
that had so much to resonate with—
those grunts, those terrible grunts
that accompanied the beat of my mother's feet.

When you listen, when you see, when you're just near
another human being, something resonates, something mirrors,
something engraves in your brain and your musculature
that you never asked for and can't get out. It has nothing
to do with will or consciousness. It just is.
And you're trapped, complicit in ways beyond bearing.
But you can't give it up, this resonance.
Everything redeeming in us as human beings comes
from the same capacity. It's what draws a mother
to a grieving child, or drew me as a mother to my son.
It's how my husband reaches me when I am
paralyzed by sorrow I will never exorcise
because it is still, *still* what will bring me back
to myself and save me.

DAY OF THE DEAD

i
This is not the day of the innocents,
it's for those who are really and truly
used, imperfect, finished, kaput.
Last year, I made an elegiac altar
to honor my valiant father-in-law
who lived a year and a half without
the other half of his heart, Joyce.
Did you see her? he would ask. *Over there
by the window? Just a flash, blue.*

In her bad times, Joyce would clamber up
the guardrails on highway bridges and, arms
spread, teeter along them like tightropes.
Ed would cry out in spite of himself,
their six children dutifully aligned behind him
but in their minds up there with her too.
Don't be an old fuddy-duddy, she'd say,
but she'd come down anyway.

In his last dreams, I wonder if she
was doing the same thing, showing him
the flip side of his own slow suicide.
She told me once she longed for the rapture.
She loved the very idea of a thrilling devotion.
Come join me, she was saying, *Come join me.*
So, for the pure irresistible thrill of her, Ed did.

ii
Yesterday, I sank to the floor felled
by this desolation that comes in the fall
like a coup de foudre I can't prepare for
or defend against. Joyce knew that place too.
Spent months after the birth of each
of her last daughters hospitalized, psychotic
with post-partum depressions. Ed never doubted
her return, patiently herded their growing brood
to church every Sunday, opened his arms
and pulled her to him when they released her.
Had his own tubes tied to protect her.

The second year of our marriage, your first wife,
drunk and sedated, choked to death.
You comforted her new husband, telling him,
There was nothing you could do. Nothing you hadn't
done already. Ambulance calls, commitments,
bail. Here I am, twenty years later, curled
on our kitchen floor, as I have been other years
in other houses, crying, but saying clearly
this time, *We* need to help me. I ask because
I have to, and I grieve for that. But I know
because you are your father's son you will.

I am nowhere near dying, nowhere near mad.
Just worn out, imperfect, something in me
finished, kaput. And you begin to pour more
heart blood in because you are the other half
of *our* heart. And I am too. So I stand up, pull
myself together, and see you off in your Spanish
wool cap, and your dead father's Disney
Day of the Dead shirt, on your dead father's birthday,
to drive seven hours to spend three watching
your granddaughter play soccer and to gift
your daughter with dividends from your parents'

inheritance. There's no point in trying to stand
between you and the pure quixotic push/pull
of these needs. But you text hourly, assuring me
of your attention, and come back to our bed
the same night. I text you a heart, a sun, a kiss,
then go upstairs to commune with my vivid,
larger than life unfinished muses, *my* after life.

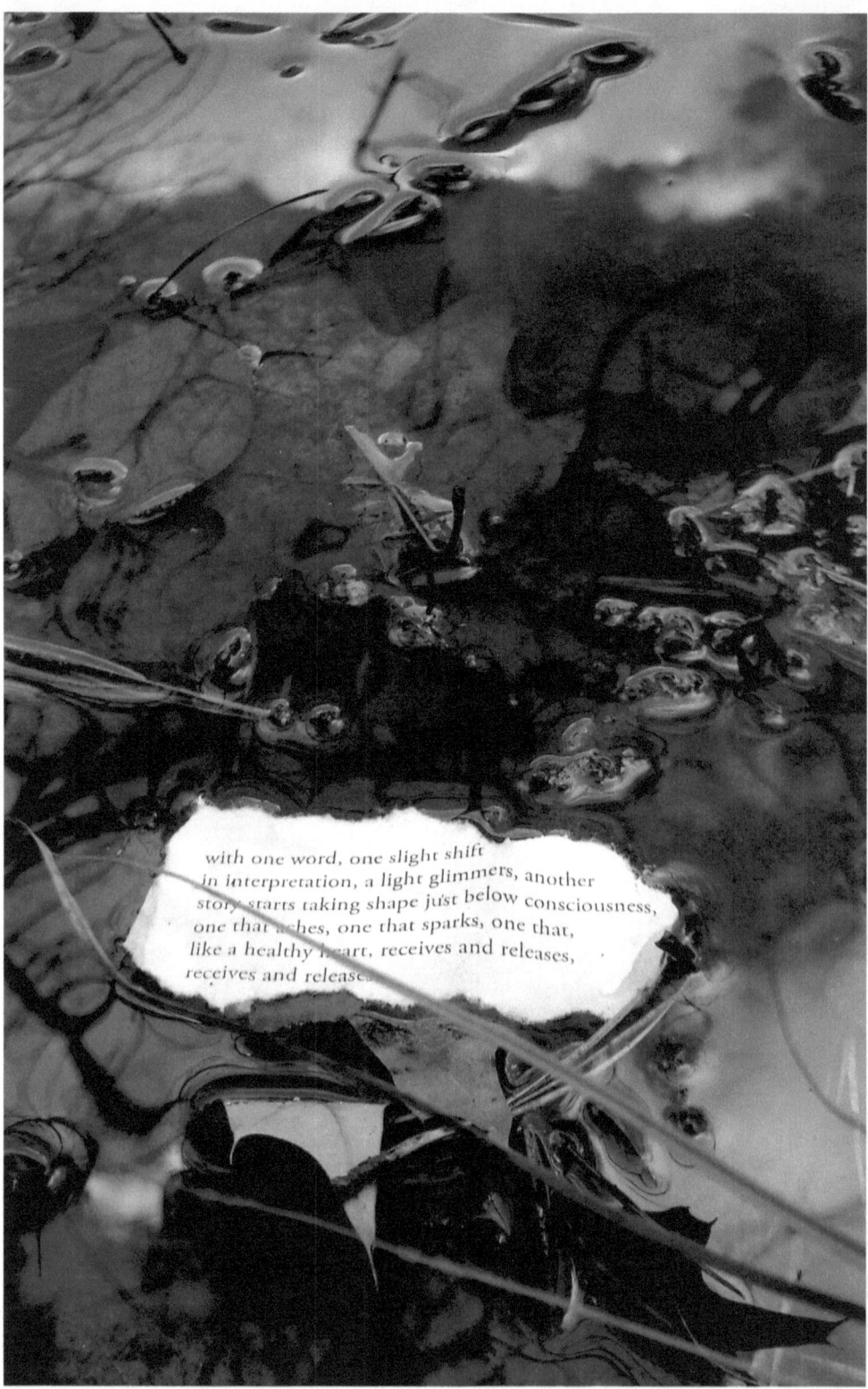

FAMILY FEELING

FAMILY FEELING

I am grieving, unexpectedly
deeply, the death of a sister
who, let's be honest about this,
never gave a thought for me.
And, honestly, I returned the favor.
Without malice. There were such gulfs
of temperament, interests—not to mention
oceans and languages and countries
between us. But here is this grief,
so keen and startling and completely
genuine for a woman of seventy-one
who closed her mouth, crossed her hands
and said, all evidence to the contrary,
"My system is done."

I don't want anyone to know yet
who might say something pro forma—
like the friend who saw her in the clinic
in Dakar a week ago and wrote us
that what our sister needed now
was to be surrounded
by the love and affection of family.
A picture so far from all our realities,
all those toxic systems and schisms,
I had nowhere to put it. But my sister,
when those words, those wishes
were read back to her, nodded.
My paranoid sister, being force-fed
through a tube that stilled her vocal cords,
nodded.

THERE IS A NEW STORY BURGEONING

There is a new story gestating, burgeoning
just under the skin,
at times it feels like a macabre,
unsightly botfly wen.

When women talk, what seems like idle chatter
is often more methodical. We're turning over—
and over and over—all the stories in our shared garden
so we can see what's hiding beneath them:
earthworms, toiling ants, hives of irascible wasps,
sprouting seeds.

Today what we're unearthing are sisters
of sisters—halfs of halfs of halfs—around the world.
They're not what we were led to expect.
They're nicer. It's almost like a coffee klatch
on WhatsApp. Greece. The Bahamas.
West Palm. Atlanta. But are we creating,
without her knowledge or consent,
my bed-ridden, wasting, voiceless
and paranoid half-sister's worst nightmare?
We're all in it together. We're all out
to get her. Get her better, we would say,
but she could feel like some terrible circle
is sealing shut, that we've encysted her,
and she's the maggot, the botfly, fighting,
yet again, for her fair share of air.

JUST LIKE EVERYONE

i
If everything we said to define ourselves
was preceded by, *Just like everyone* or
Like most of us, what would shift
in the life-long construction project
we call our self?

                    In Senegal, a sister
I've spent less than two weeks near
in fifty-six years, that's how close we are,
is starving herself to death because she believes
that she has a terrible, incurable disease
that no one will tell her about, they're all—
doctors, lover, gardener, maids, siblings
much closer than me—keeping this from her
the way they did when she was a child
with a hole in her heart and there was no
operation yet to fix it and no one would tell her why
she couldn't keep up, turned blue when she ran,
couldn't breathe, felt some dark annihilating force
gathering inside her that no one but she could see.

She's childless, but I'm not, and I wonder if I,
like most of us, like my mother, a physician herself,
would have lied, hid the prognosis given at birth:
ten years at most to live. Wouldn't it be natural
if my sister, like most of us, having overheard
someone say something in another room, would never
dare ask directly. And once she had had the operation,
that scar down her breast bone where they sawed her in half,
once she was saved from the danger they had lied, lied,
lied about even when her skin turned blue and she was

always losing at tag to her younger, favored sister,
who she hated with and for her whole heart,
wouldn't she, like most of us,
have buried all that fear, all that awful knowing,
like a corpse in her soul's garden?

ii
Do you remember England? she asked me innocently,
when I was sixteen and she had returned briefly
from her new life in Europe. Something ripped open
in me I had no words for, as if consciousness
itself had dissolved. I disappeared
into the woods for hours, returned to myself
through sight, the magenta rhododendrons
in prodigious bloom on the cliffs, and sound,
the tumbling water in the creek, and smell,
the turned dirt as I scrambled free of the path,
and pushed deeper, deeper into the trees
where no one could see. No one noticed
my absence. Even if they'd asked,
I had no way to betray myself.
No words. No memory.
Repression is a godsend.
There is a time to know,
and there is a time not to.

Thirty years later, ready for love, I was ready
to know. Void. Horror. So I could be whole,
repair the tear in my own mind, my heart.
But it has been a thirty-year retrieval project
to really see and release the many ways
that suffocating assault split and shaped me.
I drew on her, this sister who may have known,
may even have had some hand in what happened,
to create my own inner gate-keeper, so protective
and punishing, terrified, bossy, driving,
helpless, the inescapable one

who has shaped all my public speech
so it can't reach my, oh so very
mortal, core.

iii
So strange, really, that I pulled into my own psyche to save me
this angry, secretly dying girl who cut off all my curls, dressed me
like a doll, slammed a swing into my forehead. I watch my older
granddaughter, now close to the age when all this happened to me,
the way she sometimes treats her little sister when she thinks no one
is watching, and I can see its innocent reflection, understand
the power I thought I was bringing to bear to help me.
How very slight, and fierce, it really was.

Now she, my sister, just turned seventy-one, is facing a similar rip
in the veil of consciousness, convinced there is a terrible reality
the doctors are all keeping from her, or can't see.
Only she knows the truth: *No one can save me.*
"My system is through." All she can do is refuse
to fight anymore, refuse to feed her fear. So they infuse her,
kindly, with sedatives, and anti-psychotics, and multivitamins.
As if that can suppress the horror, the inescapable,
the very real horror of the truth she has known since she was born:
We are all, we are all, we are all *really* going to die.

I am not called to save her from herself
but I wonder what qualities there might have been
in the girl I once was that, drawn into her own
psyche, might help her now. Or something she
did draw in that she can let go of now.
Like the way I never, ever, saw *her* pain.

AFTERLIFE

i
She had the gusto, the pure life drive of a four year old,
the same bold, insouciant, careless heart. I don't believe
she ever held herself responsible for causing pain.
But she was filled with a wild, haunted, enraged
belief that those who were supposed to be
closest to her, her several crazy families,
were inspired by malign intent. She believed
and she raged endlessly against the belief.
I prefer that, truly, to indifference.

What I've learned in these last days,
in a vigil we mistook for a slow awakening,
as messages ringed the world from a half-
sibling here, a half-sibling there,
is that with one word, one slight shift
in interpretation, a light glimmers, another
story starts taking shape just below consciousness,
one that aches, one that sparks, one that,
like a healthy heart, receives and releases,
receives and releases.

ii
The last photo of her is almost impossible to look at,
it's so sad. I prefer to remember the virtual tour
my brother and sister gave me of her house in Dakar,
how a whole life seemed to lift into brilliant existence
when they pulled apart the shutters in her living room.
Even with the woozy camera shifts there was just enough
stability to see the masks and statues tucked into niches
in the walls, the gleaming foyer floor, the open kitchen,
the maid waving to us from the stove, the wide white-tiled
staircase our sister tumbled down just nine months before.

I insisted my younger sister grip the filigreed railing
as she climbed to our sister's bedroom, now hers
for the wake and funeral. Its closets were crammed
with beautiful robes our sister bought in sets of threes
and fours and never wore. Our mother's closet,
at her death, was similarly overwrought.
My sister momentarily reversed the camera
and I could see the pain when she described
the many bags of medicine in there too, all
stubbornly refused. I could see she was thinking,
"If I had been here—" and stopping herself.
She turned the camera toward the landing
where our dead sister's lover, preoccupied
with burial plans, waved once to yet
another total stranger.

And then, downstairs again, we, full sibs,
settled into our respective couches in Dakar, Georgia.
They brought the large tapestry behind them
into focus at my request. Antelopes,
heads high, listening, poised to react.
The camera refocused on my brother,
and we all chatted about the ocean view
from the pool at the King Fahd Hotel, about wills,

lawyers, and their trip the next day into the center
of Senegal, their regret at arriving a day too late
to say good-bye, and about this big life
our sister has lived, so peopled, so distant from our own
experience and our own experience of her.

My brother, who had felt both duty bound and terrified
at the very prospect of Senegal, had relaxed into the reality:
the squabbles with taxi drivers, the squatters compound
facing the elegant house, goats and sheep meandering
the streets, sidling up against sky scrapers. How easily
we talked, as if our own decades of estrangement
had just dissolved too. And they had, that's the odd
thing I can't get my mind around, but to which my heart
holds fast. *They have*. Just like that. Like a last breath—
Pffft—when you least expected.

Giving him a video tour of my own home
which, two decades in, he's never visited, as I
have never visited his, he remarked on the many
masks and statues I've made over the years,
how perfectly at home they'd be right there
on our dead sister's light-struck walls in Senegal.

iii
My younger sister hadn't wanted to travel into the heart of Senegal
in the same van with our sister's corpse, hadn't wanted to see it
on her arrival, didn't want to see it again. So I'm relieved
the photo she sends is of a sealed casket, blanketed with flowers,
lying in state on sawhorses in the gazebo of our sister's beloved
country home, soon to be slipped into a concrete-lined pit
in the cemetery at a small Catholic church in Sokone—
a site none of her blood relatives will ever revisit.

Seen from Google earth, the city is white with dust,
unpaved, poor—and what our sister dreamed of as her beloved,
welcoming resting place in her last bed-ridden days.
To see it is to know something we never imagined about her.
My sister tells me the church was full, the mayor spoke,
and everyone was sobbing. Afterwards, people came up
to tell her how our sister had found them jobs, flown
their children to Rome for treatment. It's true,
they're grieving, deeply, someone we never knew.

iv
At four in the morning, the hour they rolled her casket
into the van, I woke hyper-ventilating, in tears.
It is a grief so complicated that this is the only way
it can reach me or I it. I don't even know how much
it has to do with her. It has to do with that last picture
received two weeks ago, the one I haven't had the courage
to look at twice. Hours later, going through my photo archives,
as random and over-stuffed as my sister's closets, I find
no visual record of her after 1971. I can count on one hand
the number of times I saw her since. What I remember
most is how she would physically get too close, encroach
on you when she was talking. I was always shrinking back.
She was always pressing in, always urgent.

Now I take that last photo in with steadied gaze.
Her hands, the right intubated, the left not,
one flaccid, slightly clawed. I just see the shape
of them and my whole being aches, there's such
a relinquishment. I know I don't want that for her.
Even in the afterworld, I *want* her urgency, her need
to be included. I'm so tired of keeping that need
in me at a distance, retreating from it
just as instinctively as I retreated from her.
So on this day of her burial, as she permanently
releases it, I breath in her wild urgency,
her insistence that life is a feast and we all
have a place at it, even if we have to shove
a little to get in there.

v
We can only accept in others what we
have made a space for in ourselves.
That's all I've learned recently—
that I am a hologram and don't need
to keep weaving and reweaving a consistent
story, it's all there, it's *always* all there.
And I'm a multitude as well,
that is what my sister's death is teaching me
simultaneously, that there is no point in trying
to define ourselves as *not* someone, somewhere,
sometime. They've all gotten in, gotten under our skin,
become part of our own synapses.
That's what it means to be human.

This sister, whose bossy, instinctively cruel
ways as a child I borrowed and used to control
my own fissured soul for decades, I'm releasing her
so I can let the real woman in, with all her own
fissures and urgencies and life force and long, long history
that hasn't a single blessed thing to do with me.
Wandering here, in my own soul's garden, turning over
this stone, turning over that one, I wonder what drama,
chaos, turbulence and zest she will bring with her.

I'm bringing in too this image of her that it has taken me
weeks to be able to stare at steadily—bed-ridden, passive,
suspicious or just puzzled, determined to be seen, recorded
as is, as is . . . I can't help wondering what is coming into being
as we both accept that helplessness—a state we've each fought
off fiercely all our lives. I hope the story is one that will release us,
release her from all those claustrophobic stories I've been telling
myself about her—and release me from how brutally
they have bound me too.

These aren't rooms we're renting, they are world views that seep through our skin as we sleep.

LIFE IN TRANSLATION

REGRESAREMOS

I'll come back from my travels
mute, everything that really mattered
soaring above or sinking below speech.
So how will anyone know what's shifted,
how deeply, or how permanently?
Regresaremos, we've been saying
whenever we have an experience
that breaks through that austere
numbness of travel. *Regresaremos*
we say to anyone who will listen.
It means something, these words,
not just to us but to those
receiving them, sure as we are
return is already, in this simple
phrasing, taking place. Turn
and turn again, home
is always defined,
and redefined,
by what lies beyond it.

OAXACA, DECEMBER 2014

i
The weather couldn't be more perfect here,
air just cool enough, breeze frequent enough
we can bask in bright sun for hours
placid as *tortugas*.

Agua! Agua!
The calls from the street are more
regular than the calls from minarets.
As are the ones from the plaza.
Ayotzinapa!
Ayotzinapa!

At breakfast we read feeds from the New York Times.
To speak, the father of one of the disappeared
steadies himself with a thimble of mezcal.
"All I want is for someone
to have left him
alone in a field
so they could
return to me
his little bones.
That would be
a consolation."
Sus huesitos.
Mi consuelo.

¡Vivos se los llevarnos!
Bring them back to us alive.
¡Vivos se los llevarnos!
Agua agua

Ayotzinapa
Agua agua
Ayotzinapa

We haven't made our way yet
to the zócalo where men stand
three deep reading pages of *Imparcial*
strung up on clothes pins. It is all there,
in color, waving above the papaya
and panela. Burning trucks
in the isthmus, young men macheted
for their cellphones, a son buried
in the patio by a father still drunk with horror
who thinks no one but he will notice
the absence.

The father doesn't think, like the mayor
and the narcotraficantes in Guerrero,
to burn his son first to ash, blend him with
polvo, the endless dust that season after season,
they seed and till. Perhaps somewhere in him
he still believes on the third day there will be
an upheaval, the stones on the patio will move
in *misericordia,* such miraculous
misericordia, and his son will stand
before him again, breathing, letting any doubting
Thomas probe the wounds, signs of a father's
pura locura and vicious *impotencia,*
and call those terrible *heridas* love.

¡Vivos se los llevarnos!
Bring them back to us alive.
¡Vivos se los llevarnos!
Agua agua
Ayotzinapa
Agua agua
Ayotzinapa

ii
It's stenciled all over the city.
Queremos vivos
Scrawled on all the walls.
Ayotzinapa
Ayotzinapa
Queremos los 43 desaparecidos.
Queremos vivos.
We want them alive.

Day and night, a voice recites
the names of the lost in an endless loop
in an empty patio in *El Museo de Arte
Contemporanea*. Imprecation, invocation.
I listen, record, move on.

It's the drooping clothesline in the zócalo,
the photos waving like prayer flags
that bring me to a full stop.
They're so young, these aspiring
teachers, hijacked and shot
while they themselves were hijacking buses
in a good cause, they thought. The givens
are so hard to sort out.
The loss, the absolute loss is not.

All spring, summer, and fall
in my own country I have listened
to men who have lost ten, twenty,
thirty, even forty years behind bars,
listened to them trying to make, at our request,
sense, good sense, of it all.
The givens are so hard to sort out.
The loss, the absolute loss, is not.

iii
We're here in the month of the virgins,
Juquila, Guadalupe, Soledad, Santissima
Madre, Maria. The whole town parades,
throws candy, shimmies inside festive gigantes,
carves creches and horses and Zapotec
gods from tubers big as manioc for the night
of the radishes, *La Noche de los Rabanos*.
The city leaders are negotiating with the teachers
now occupying the plaza to protest the imposition
of any performance standards, the loss of their sinecures,
and the irreparable loss of the *desaparecidos*.
What are they teaching, with their tidy pup tents,
their prayer flags with the faces of dead boys too young to vote,
their marches on the capital, their torching of buses,
their failure to teach, their entitlement and grief hopelessly
snarled together, like hair from a common hair brush
or a weaver's discarded thread?

¡Vivos se los llevarnos!
¡Vivos se los llevarnos!
Agua agua
Ayotzinapa
Agua agua
Ayotzinapa

iv
Los queremos regresar. Regresar vivos.
Los queremos vivos.

Like *¡Agua! ¡Agua!*, it is a call
to prayer we can all join in.
Los respuestos, though, startle
like the fireworks for the Virgin of Juquila,
loud as gunshots, echoing back and forth
between the hazy mountains.
We flinch. Next time it could be us.
And we don't want to be defined by that why,
or why not, which is so miserably small,
so invincibly terrible, and just
the same stuff as we are.

In the church services I've been attending
up north and down south all the prayers
begin with fervor and confidence.
Father God, Padre Nostre, we ask you—
and I hear, as they do so, chains falling,
but I always flinch and make the transposition
that eases me like these cries
of *¡Agua! ¡Agua!, ¡Ayotzinapa!*
Fallen God, *Fallen* God, *Fallen* God,
we pray—

For the boys, *los desaparecidos,* who won't ever teach—
For the teachers who could if they would—
For the son who won't rise from the dead—
For the father who must console himself with a single shard
of bone, who knows its most human name is one he gave it—
For the mother who poisoned her comatose daughter
who would never wake and then herself
so they would never be separated—

For the mothers of Central America marching
to mark the years their migrant children
have disappeared without a trace—
lost somewhere between Huehuetenango,
Tegucigalpa, Oaxaca, Ayotzinapa, Monterey, and San Diego—
For the brown boys at home imprisoned for a lifetime
at fifteen, so reasonably raging against their disappearance,
raging for second, third or tenth chances, for literacy,
an unobstructed view, a woman's touch,
those boys who I, even now, am trying to put,
just like that mad father did his own flesh and blood,
out of sight, out of mind.

Fallen God, *Fallen* God,
Los queremos regresar. Regresar vivos.
Los queremos vivos.

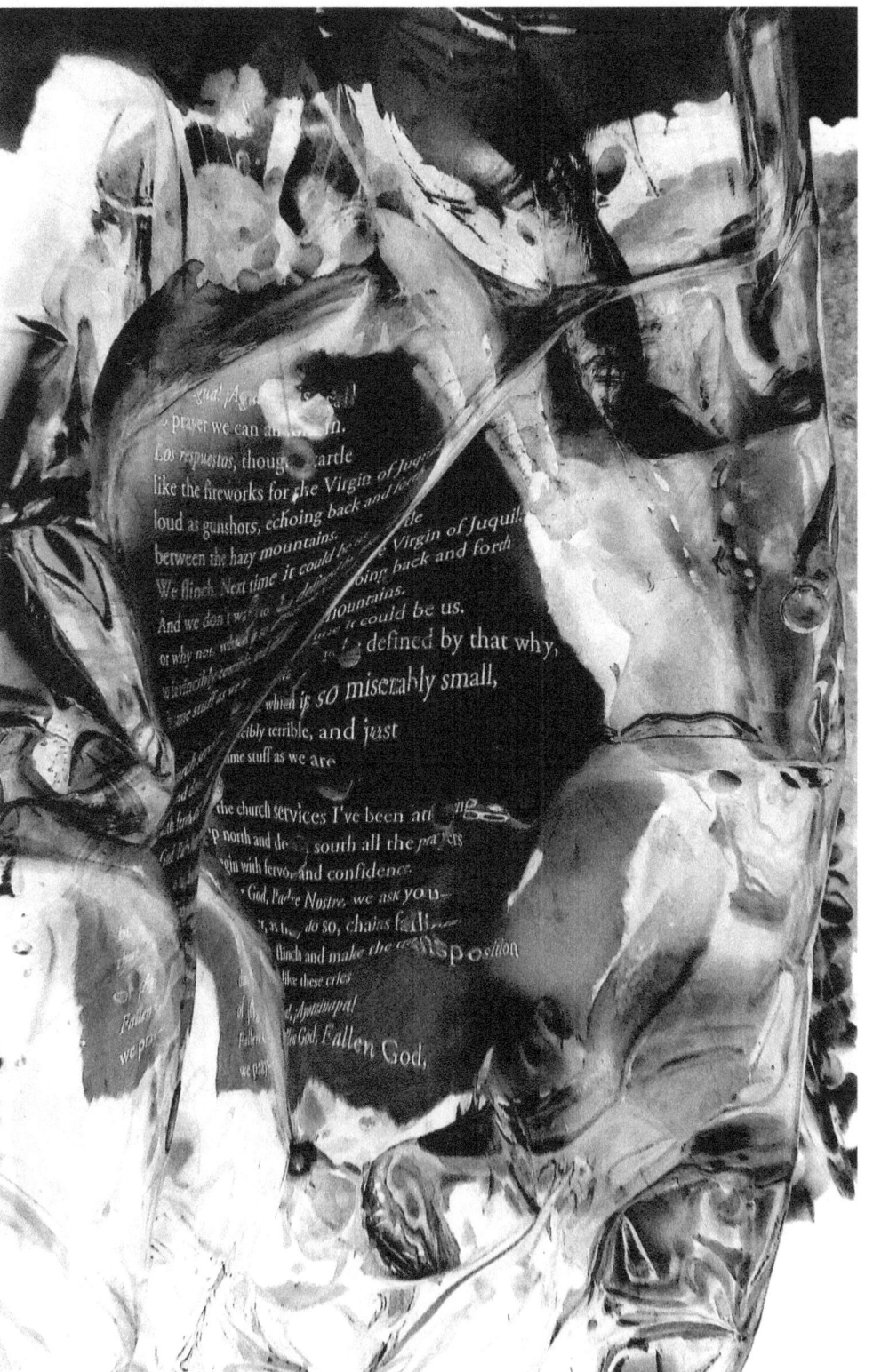

DEPARTURE

Light expands like a sleeper's breath
into a high walled patio. I'm still here
to receive it. Lemon trees shiver
twelve feet above my head
on someone else's solid ground.
A strand of ivy wavers in a lilt of wind,
sliding between two inverted roof tiles
fashioned into monkish figures
who patiently wait to see who and what
comes after me. Eight days
is long enough to habituate, to feel
uprooted when we leave. I am,
always and everywhere, a homing pigeon.
I grieve.

NOW NÃO NOW NÃO

Is it always like this, words
coming only as the train pulls out,
the airplane rears and rises?
We see, really see, for a flash second—
and want to live in that holy hologram
we glimpsed in the turn of a head,
or a pilfered phrase—like a bell wants to live
in that amazing vibration that has nothing
to do with its own dense, smelted reality.
Now. *Não*. Now. *Não*. Now.

LIFE IN TRANSLATION

The fifth home in four weeks is the last straw.
La quinta casa in quattro settimane è l'ultima goccia.

These aren't rooms we're renting, they are world views that seep through our skin as we sleep.
Queste non sono le stanze che stiamo affittando, sono visioni del mondo che penetrano attraverso la nostra pelle mentre dormiamo.

They steep in our imagination.
Ripidono nella nostra immaginazione.

I've had enough.
Ho avuto abbastanza.

I don't want to know how much care went into choosing the red-checked napkins to match the red plates, the exact arrangement of dried toasts and tea on the tray. Where her husband works—creating mosaic tiles only streets away—and how her daughter came to do development work among the poor of El Salvador. Or what shocked, lured, and exhilarated her niece when she visited Indonesia. Or when these cruise ships started towering over Piazza San Marco.

Non voglio sapere quanta attenzione è stata posta nella scelta dei tovaglioli a quadretti rossi per abbinarli ai piatti rossi, alla disposizione esatta dei toast secchi e del tè sul vassoio. Dove lavora suo marito—creando tessere di mosaico solo a una certa distanza—e come sua figlia è venuta a fare lavori di sviluppo tra i poveri di El Salvador. O che cosa ha scioccato, adescato ed euforico sua nipote quando ha visitato l'Indonesia. O quando queste navi da crociera iniziarono a torreggiare su Piazza San Marco.

Of course that's not true. I want to seep into their imaginations, I never want them to leave mine. I want to trust my memory to retain enough trace of them that four months or a year from now some small detail will prick my consciousness sharp as a safety pin, a thorn, and wake me permanently.

QUEM TEM ALMA NÃO TEM CALMA

i
It may just be a woman thing,
this momentary infatuation I had with Pessoa,
during my ten days in Lisboa.
A single line or two and I locked in.
Não sei quantas almas tenho.
      I don't know how many souls I have
Cada momento mudei—
      Each moment I changed—

I sighed with recognition
when I reached,
Quem tem alma não tem calma.
I thought I'd found someone,
a man no less, who also slipped in
and out of sensibilities the way I do,
losing myself in other physiologies, points of view.
Someone who knew how involuntary, how unsettling
but necessary this soul travel is.

Just writing this down now takes me somewhere
I don't want to go, somewhere
I'm doing everything I can to avoid—
The mind of the girl with eyes
closed tight trapped in an alley in Pamplona,
men on every side crowding in.
Quem tem alma não tem calma.

ii
Days later, I would wonder, heartsick,
how could I have misread him so?
Pessoa doesn't move from soul to soul.
It all comes back to him in the end,
all these 67 or 78 hierononyms
that scholars dutifully catalogue.
All those alters—Caeiro, Reis, Campos, Soares,
Deus também—are just so many ways
to keep the attention on himself.
Like the face he made up as a woman's
just so it could meet his own lips in the mirror.
There is only one self-besotted personality here.
Quem tem alma não tem calma.

How could I have misread him so?
Just when did the claustrophobia,
the recognition come in?
Was it the very day we arrived in Spain?
The day of that inconceivable decision?
After months of deliberation, a judge
saw only blameless revelry, animal spirits,
in the hands of all those young men groping, probing,
tearing away the consciousness of a terrified girl
trapped in an alley in Pamplona.

Despite the outcry of thousands of women,
the judge felt tranquil, supported by the good wishes
of fellow judges, his family, at ruling
these young men be completely absolved of responsibility.
The law requires force and resistance. He saw neither in all
those many groping hungry hands, her dissociated passivity.
Quem tem alma não tem calma.

I can't help but wonder what his own wife felt
when she realized that all these years he's understood
nothing, absolutely nothing about her,
that if she packed her bags and left,
he would still see nothing where she—
who *has* a soul, who *has* no calm—can see
the horror of those hands so implacably in love
with their own lust they know nothing,
absolutely nothing, of the hells they create.

Does she see, like me, see the lips of the woman
in Pessoa's mirror open into a scream?

I am, through... rough every c...
with the ... he raw but inn... God.
... the G... God you haven... ...illed out
who pulle... pulled out the nails,
the arro... rows, dropped the cross,
killed the u... the unborn, unwanted child
the God wh... d who knows what it is to...
... man's carna...
freed of man... he world in...
remake the ... nough. Yes is v... free
Enough is en... ... Yes is yes. No...

VOICES IN A SEVILLA NIGHT

1

They couldn't help themselves,
I tell my sister, my neighbors.
It was the alcohol, the excitement
of the bulls. Their need to show off
to each other. And she didn't tell them
not to. She was wearing a short skirt,
wasn't she? Leggings, they correct me,
but that is as if she were half-naked,
asking them to imagine her in that way.
I defend them, it's true, but when I go
to the jail to visit with my son, I can't
look him in the eye. Something rises in me,
something rank and bitter. Something that
has no place in a mother. He thinks
he is being treated unfairly. His father
and uncle do too. They talk in low voices
but the anger, the righteousness are there
in how they push their shoulders back,
hold their heads up, daring anyone not
to meet their gaze. It makes me more than tired.

I sign up to teach another class
and tell my husband he will need to visit
for the two of us. He needs you, my husband
protests. The defense feels it's important to show
he has close relationships with women.
Like a terrorist has warm ties with his mother?
I ask. Our son is not a terrorist, my husband says.
We stare at each other, my husband
and I, daring each other to find a word
we can, either of us, hide behind.

2

He's a brute, I tell my father.
He's your brother, he tells me.
I will never look at him again, I say.
His name will never cross my lips.
That *is* a vow.
It's just the way of young men, he says.
They take orders from their coronels.
They follow their friends the same way
they chase the bulls. It's raw but innocent.
So you know how he was feeling
when he choked that girl with his prick?
I ask him. When his four friends did the same.

Watch your language, he tells me. He looks dazed,
frightened, but that does not stop me any more
than those same expressions stopped my brother.
Why not watch the movie, I tell him.
The whole world has. Why can't you see
with *their* eyes, *my* eyes. *My brother
is vile.* The judge says there was no violence,
my father protests. She did not speak. She did not
bite the flesh that filled her mouth. This, the judge
insists, absolves them completely. They should go free.
My father looks ten years older today than he did yesterday,
which was ten years older than he was the day before.
He has the mercy of Methuselah. I do not.
I want to tear my brother's heart out
and make my father eat it. I have inside me
the purest rage at the world he's brought me into.

I am, through every cell, filled
with the raw but innocent fury of God,
of the God you haven't met yet,
who pulled *out* the nails, pulled *out*

the arrows, dropped the cross,
killed the unborn, unwanted child,
the God who knows what it is to be a woman
freed of man's carnage, free to wreak her own,
remake the world in *her* image. Whatever the cost.
Enough is enough. Yes *is* yes. No *is* no.
They are, by the thousands, shouting this in the streets
and I am shouting it now in my own home.

My father hides his face in his hands.
I can hear his tears slipping through his thick,
calloused fingers, the ones that taught my brother
how to change a light bulb, mend a pipe,
tune a motor, fill out his application
for the *guardia civil*. How can you ever
defend him, I ask, after what your own mother
went through? He covers his head
as if my words are stones. When she was dying,
she told me, you know. Where you came from,
how she would never know who your father was
because there were so many who had had their way.
At that he straightens. Speaks with the voice
of a small boy, something eerie and pure.
My father was a hero.
I did not know until that moment exactly
what my grandmother had saved him from.
Her only child, a son.

I remember as if it were yesterday, she told me,
I see every face, all those grimaces, hear the laughter
as they entered and left, the sound
of their hands slapping each other's shoulders.
I have pondered each one of them in my heart
like a message from another world. Every day,
all these years. She looked at me, her face creased
like used paper, but the smile that of an irrepressible
girl. I am their living hell, she whispered. The saints
help me. They send messages back to them,

ones that will wake them at night as they enter
their wives, ones that will stab them
in their hearts when they hold their daughters
for the first time, ones that will make them writhe
on their death beds. All is not and never will be
forgiven. I pray for their impotence, for
heart attacks and cancer and terrifying dementias
where they find themselves trapped inside
my body, seeing each one of their comrades
grimacing over them, hearing the sound of those hands
slapping backs, the laughter coming and going,
feel, with each thrust, what it really means
to extinguish a soul. This is why I light candles
every day. This is what frees me to love
your father. When I die, *nieta mia*, you will be
my living memory. It will be your turn to haunt them.
Every day, without fail. Promise me.

Just like your mother, I tell my father,
until my dying day, I will call on all the saints,
all the violated virgins, to relieve
this woman of the sin
that is your son, my brother.

3

I go every day and kiss his bound hands
and cross myself and return
to the back of the line because once
is not enough to relieve
what pierces me again and again
and again and again, this terrible
love I have for my only son.
For two years now, I have asked
El Señor de la Sentencia to help me
bear what his own father never had to—
shame. Each time I go to the prison
my son asks me how long he will have to wait
to learn his fate. I want to tell him,
"The blood will never dry on the innocent forehead
of El Señor de la Sentencia. Why do you
think it should dry on yours?"
There is remorse on the blameless face
of the son of God, but my son's face
blushes sometimes with rage, blanches
with fear, but is untouched by remorse.
He always meets my eyes. Never looks away.
After the first time, I've never let him try
to explain. "Of course she knew what she
was in for. How couldn't she?"

These words are *my* cross. These words
are *my* sentence. And still, I go to the prison
as regularly as I go to mass.
My daughter thinks I have absolved
my son. She couldn't be more wrong.
I would kill a man who did anything
like this to her. I would kill *all* of them.
And still I love him unbearably, with his warm
brown shameless eyes, his curls as wild

as my mother's, with the soft lips of my wife,
and my hands—he has *my* hands.
I can't get that out of my mind, so every day
I kneel before El Señor and kiss *his* hands,
he who knows what *his* father has done to him,
knows the cost that he, the innocent,
is being asked to pay, knows it
and still loves the source of his torment.

HOARDING

It's not self-abnegation, this pleasure
I take in erasing all traces of my presence
from spaces I've filled to the brim
for days on end with mystical intuitions,
shopping lists, fresh bread, té de ortiga,
novels by Rosa Montero and poems by Rafael Alberti,
maps of Sevilla, Cadíz, Granada,
pastry from the TajHalal, brochures from shows
on Miguel Hernandez, Murillo, Yoko Ono,
Dinh Q Lê, sombreros of paper from China
molded to look like straw that dissolve when brushed
by a raindrop—and clippings, so many clippings,
of La Manada, Sevilla's homeboys,
and copy cat gang rapes in Santiago, Chile.

I take in our last laundry set out on a drying rack
on a narrow balcony overlooking Pagés del Corro,
and sweep away the bougainvillea leaves
that keep sailing in, nestling deep in the corners,
such vivid reminders of lives unseen.
I pack computers and cameras holding images
of people and *pasajes* caught in passing,
so many Madonnas rolling their eyes,
so may sons of God lolling, mortified,
on their laps, engraved walls the color of ivory
that still hold the calls to prayer of exiled imams,
wilting bouquets, hundreds of them,
tumbled before a small scabbed statue of San Judas de Tadeo,
a white handkerchief waving from a balcony
in the evening breeze, the words scrawled there
forming and reforming, *Sí, te creo.*

I've done this packing up, sweeping away,
setting things back exactly the way I found them
more times times than all the years I've lived.
But each time I stand that last time
at the doorway, retrace in memory
my last attentive visit to each room, each
emptied drawer, emptied cupboard, washed plate,
I don't feel erased. I feel all accounted for:
Hands, heart, eyes, mind, *all*
mine. Again.

SONG FOR THE FAINT OF HEART AND MISALIGNED

We find time to touch the kiwi,
fresas, y albaricoche, to bend
and smell them, to feel washed clean
in the wave of sound from the Bar de Trebol
on the corner of Calle Abades and Embajadores,
which, in just hours, has begun to feel like home.

The floors of the narrow balconies slant
like worn shoes and across the street
a woman sits on her bed half-dressed,
her stretched legs plump and sturdy.
She slips in and out of focus between
the clothes pinned across three laundry lines.
If she looked up she could see us just as clearly.

A white mannequin two balconies down
stands sentry, like an archangel
on a slow day. *¡Mentira!* a tattered poster
on the far side of the street protests.
Anarchy is not *desorden, confusión
por falta de autoridad*. It is, instead,
*autogestión, internationalismo,
ateísmo, solidaridad, sentido critico,
compromiso, coherencia, acción directa,
desobediencia.*

¡Organízate y lucha!
we are ordered sternly.
How dare we disobey?
The words fall so easily into rhythm.
Des-des-des-o-be-dien-ci-a
co-co-co-her-en-ci-a
au-to-au-to-ges-tión,
au-to-au-to-ges-tioooooónnnnnnn!

PURA VIDA

i
¡Pura vida!
What *does* it mean?
The answer is always a shrug.
The best. The worst.
Nothing. Everything.

¡Pura vida!
It took less than a minute
to unburden us of nearly all
we carried that day. So there
we were, undeniably old,
but not yet that forgetful,
walking up and down the aisle
of the emptied bus, querying
each empty seat, interrogating
the empty spaces beneath them,
receiving the same answer.
Nadanadanadanada

The driver just shrugged.
We kept going back over and over
how it could have happened.
Was it that moment you slipped
across the aisle to make eye contact
with him, to ask how soon we'd reach the end
of the line, the place we would head back from
when the day was done. Asking because
we are always thinking ahead.

So there we were, the end of the line, left with nothing
but your collapsible fedora, the clothes on our backs,
the contents of our pockets. They took sunblock,
bathing suits, long pants and shirts for our return,
your iphone, and, worst, our electronic books.
A full day in this hot, sleepy, perfectly
illiterate beach town and nothing to read.
¡Qué pesadilla!
Ningún periódico. Ningún libro.
Nadanadanada para leer.
Except menus and pricetags on beachwear.
¡Pura vida!
¡Pura vida!

ii
Nowhere else in the world have I been robbed.
But here, twice, twenty years apart.
Does that make a habit, *una costumbre?*
Twenty-one years ago, newly married, one slash
of a razor as I bent to collect my suitcase
and everything that identified me disappeared.
I spent days stranded without money, passport,
not a single person I knew in the whole city,
you out of contact in the mountains.

For years I kept remembering that razor.
How I wept when I handed over my very last dollars
to replace my passport. How, hearing the birds
singing at four in the morning, harbingers
of sunrise, I covered my ears, felt that new gold ring
digging into my earlobe and wondered what on earth
I'd gotten myself into. For years I couldn't forget the pure
dread that had nothing to do with the loss of property,
nothing to do with the intentions of the man who slashed off
my travel pack, just the *idea* of the razor, the vicious edge of it,
just the reality of my own skin, how thin it was—and still is.
I didn't see it coming. I didn't feel it when it was there.
¡Pura vida!

iii
¡Pura vida!
But this time we're together. It's not a week, it's a day trip.
We count our cash. The bus ticket is reissued. You peer
into every trash can in town hopeful they kept the electronics
but discarded the knapsack still holding our clothes, and perhaps,
perhaps, our reading matter. What will they do
with *The Book of Disquiet, Poesía imprescindible,*
Essays in Radical Empiricism or *The Varieties of Religious Experience*—
with *Love in a Time of Cholera, Brevísima relación de la destrucción de las*
Indias or *Incidents in the Life of a Slave Girl Written by Herself?*
And what will we do without them?

You check under every palm tree on Playa Jaco, while I cool my feet
in the surf and lift my spirits by composing elaborate curses to rain down
on the impenitent heads of our sneak thieves, their parents, grandparents,
innocent children, and the children of those innocent children.
We buy a radiant pareo to cover our bare knees on the cold bus home.
"And they returned," I say twisting the key in the lock to our apartment,
"with nothing but the clothes on their backs . . . " And hearts filled
with *maldiciones*, still looking for a face, a name, one specific history
to settle our wrath and blame on. Failing that, we say,
Pinche, pinche, maldito país.

iv
But we can't leave it at that. Despite our righteous indignation,
we remember the zen-like concentration of the young man
who blow-torched the cheese on the tops of our crepes,
the endearing pride with which he served us. *¡Pura vida!*
The taste of blackberries, so rich and so sweet,
in the cold sorbet we bought before returning to the beach.
¡Pura vida! The relief of those waves washing over my scorched feet
when I reached the ocean's edge and began showering vengeance
yet again on those *ladrones,* those *sin vergüenzas,* who were,
let's be honest about this, no more intentional than the young boys
who burgled us of far worse in Atlanta—a new car, four computers.
These thieves too had no real need, just a keen, irresistible sense
of opportunity. The way just passing you might pluck a papaya
from a low hanging branch. Just because it was there.
Because my head was turned.
Because their passing bodies blocked your view.
It took no more time or thought than breathing in, out.
Why not?

¡Pura vida!
¡Pura vida!

v
The young banker with a round face, earnest mien,
asks me what language I want to use to express
my distress. Yesterday, young thugs robbed us
in Jaco, now, a day later, the *cajero automatico* in San José
slurped back my bankcard like a lizard would a fly.
"*Me robó*," I say. "*Su banco me robó.*"
For reasons of security, he tells me again,
you have only thirty seconds to retrieve it.
It seems they have time-tested the agility of local thieves.

The bank, he adds softly, usually needs a week to release it.
Tears pour from under my sunglasses. I won't leave
without something in writing that acknowledges
my loss, gives me clear instructions on how to regain
some modicum of control. The young man disappears
behind dark doors. We stand there waiting, you stoic,
my eyes running eternally like Rilke's fountain.
Pinche, pinche, pinche maldito país.

A fellow American pauses in front of us but doesn't
make eye contact. He's covered with tattoos, smoking,
overweight, in shorts and a t-shirt. A long chain, thicker
than his big stub thumb, loops from back pocket
to the back of his knee. It anchors his wallet.
He doesn't seem aware of the automatic tellers,
the people lined up to use them, the city,
perhaps even the century. But no one can take his
pinche wallet without taking him along too.
This is an answer of sorts. *¡Pura vida!*

The banker returns with map, instructions, apologies
for those few of his countrymen who are less than good,
promises to do everything he can to help us.
He does not want us to think poorly of his beautiful country.
While he speaks and I weep, our spaced out compatriot
weaves blindly down the street. *¡Pura vida!*

vi
True to his word the banker calls the next afternoon.
He's worked a miracle. The card is ours if we can get there
before closing time. It's a race, but everyone obliges.
The taxista, the assiduous clerks who call all over the bank,
walk its halls, stay overtime, serve us cappuccinos and cookies
to keep our hopes up, while a Nicaraguan guard confides
his love for our great compatriot, Walt Whitman.
We leave at dusk, relieved, our card in hand.
Gracias all around.

As usual at this hour to the east dark clouds threaten,
but to the west the sky expands, a pure, limitless blue.
Inside our apartment, bedrooms facing east, living room
facing west, you can never see both views at once.
You have to choose. We choose to remember the sweet
taste of the cappuccino, the guard raising his arms in joy
as he told us how our great poet's words filled him
with the courage to find his own.

¡Pura vida!
¡Pura vida!

PENETRATION

i
They're a decade old,
these magazines decorously arranged
through the apartment: *Vanidades,*
*Cosmopolitan*s and *Su Casa*s,
and, tucked tidily below them,
two porno magazines. I've never
opened one before, something
that at sixty-eight bemuses me.
I do so now because I'm looking
for nudes for collages I want to create.
In the first, the women are all bikinied
and no use to me, the cloth
blurs body lines. In the second,
the emphasis is unrelentingly
genital, except they are trying
to make appeasing narratives
with large italicized sidebars
about how a woman wants to be
entered every way imaginable.
The subtext is the bonding between men
who have found themselves a willing,
absolving receptacle. They are all,
Wendy, Willy, and Andy,
on a first name basis. Every woman
is arranged so her shaved pubis and air-brushed
labia and vagina are visible. Most of the time
she is on her knees, looking coyly
back over her shoulder, one leg raised
like a male dog, the better to show her sex.
Sometimes she is on her back, opening
herself with her own fingers, her tongue

suggestively touching her upper lip.
I've read that young woman these days
stage their vaginas like their houses,
use low lighting, a selfie stick.

ii
But for someone like me, who knew
far too early what it felt like to be
throttled, suffocated by another's flesh,
what I can't get over is the subtext
of vacuous willingness staged by men.
What on earth did these women really feel
when they posed? What would they feel now
a decade later, if they opened one of these
dusty, scuffed magazines and saw their younger selves
looking back at them, so vapid, sly?

There's nothing here for me, I think, flipping
quickly with the rapacious focus of the artist
on a quest. Then one image stops me,
a penis, engorged, on the verge of penetration.
As purely genital as you can get, but
there is something different about the quality
of the lighting, something I do need to see
and receive if I am ever to be freed
of what those early assaults did to me.
I take that one image, the tension
of it, the simplicity of the raw flesh
and something else that the homoerotic photographer,
or the happenstance of light, gave it—
something about true yearning, the true power
to receive, and the life that, in turn, arises from it,
about what these decades of your sweet,
patient, steady but unassuming
desire have created in me, of what we,
flesh to flesh, equally graced, still invite
and are invited to.

I close the magazine, consider trashing it,
but tuck it instead at the bottom of the stack,
just below the tamer one with the bikinied
lovelies, which is topped in turn by the *Cosmopolitan*
in Spanish hyping surgically refined vaginas.
I try to imagine why our attractive blonde landlady
from Belarus in her body hugging lycra—who handily
crawls on top of the dryer on the back porch,
buttocks suggestively raised,
to attach netting to keep out the pigeons;
who has a golf-playing sugar daddy from Kentucky
but mows her own square yard of lawn;
and whose one book shelf holds only books on money
and word etymologies—keeps these glossy, old, obscene
magazines for her visitors, and has her demure
Nicaraguan maid straighten them weekly.
What world is *she* righting?

WAYS OF MOVING THROUGH THE WORLD

The lilt in the walk of Francisco Zúñiga's women
does not belong here in his *país natal*,
rather in his adopted country, in Juchitán,
where bold thick-waisted women
in bright flowing skirts joust
provocatively with aging white men
who stop to buy tamales or an aguacate,
laughing as the color rises in pale lined cheeks
when they jut their breasts and shake their hips
and say, ¡*Tan guapo, güero! ¿Quieres mas?*
The bold smiles and bolder laughter ricochet
throughout the mercado as everyone shares
the simple pleasure, given and received, of being seen—
at whatever age—as fully ripe.

The three women here in the sculpture garden in San José
keep walking into their disparate futures
with that same brazen lilt, but the rain and the birds
have etched their faces with something more
somber, silent. And yet they feed me in a way this city
with its *ropas americanas* on every corner,
its modest, caged houses, rubbled sidewalks,
groaning buses, relentless sunshine and ready wind,
its miles and miles of spiraled barbed wire do not.

In el parque nacional, another Zúñiga, Edgar, who shares
a father with Francisco, but is a generation younger, creates
equally monumental statues of men effortfully
unearthing themselves, like so many tragic
reiterations, their arms all stretched in supplication,
their legs still entangled below ground. They know
what it's like never to sever your ties with the land
of your birth, the effort required simply to kneel upon it.

But these women, seen with an emigré's eyes, walk easily,
heads erect, eyes fixed fearlessly on the horizon, becoming one
with the gravitational pull of both the earth and the stars.
They invite me to a similar stance, a similar rhythm,
where I discover a lightness of bearing, a strength of being,
that comes from heading straight into the unknown, heart first.
The only question is, can I take it home with me?

FOOTPRINTS IN THE AIR

In that space between languages
our senses do our thinking and random
movement entrains our ideas now and then.
Huellas en el aire is how a choreographer
describes the live, evanescent dance
performances to which he has dedicated
his professional life. Like making love, they exist
only in the moment. His hobby is concretizing,
remodeling houses, choosing every detail,
color scheme, window shape, then
handing it off to a relative or friend
so he can begin again.

Everything comes back to *re*-membering
our lives, collecting what floats unbidden
into consciousness: the shape of a woman's head
in the concert audience last night, so sweetly round,
hair just beginning to return after chemo.
The way she tipped it back, swiveled in her seat
entraining with the beat, such radiance as she sang
along with the band she's listened to for forty years,
casting a warm glance at her friend to her left,
her husband to her right, with every breath
absorbing and releasing pure joy—
the way, this morning, my own cells
wordlessly receive, release,
memories of her. *Huellas.*
Huellas. Such beautiful traces
of grace.

ENTRAINING WITH THE HOLY

i
So this is where it begins,
the fullness of age,
the breathing in and holding fast
and absorbing. The savoring
in situ. No better place to be
than here on a rooftop in Valparaíso,
where when you look out or up,
it's there, the promise of the infinite.
And when you look down
it's a hard-scrabble town
with roofs and walls of tin,
vivid murals and furious
slogans, *estado asesino,*
muerte a Piñera,
and carpets of raw garbage
leading to a cobbled plaza
filled with fresh *uvas* and ripe tomatoes,
fresas, duraznos y duraznos duros, pepinos,
hierbas medicinales, sponges, toilet paper
toothpaste, soap.

All the faces of the statues weep red.
Metal doors block plundered stores.
When asked, a young woman smiles, tells us,
the closest supermarket was ransacked,
the second burned, but the third, *sí,*
es abierto. The way it's said, it feels like a single
pilgrimage—that we can't get to the open one
without genuflecting before the others first.
We hesitate, keep finding other excursions to take.
We're riding all the historic *ascensores,* those
inertial elevators, one rising while the other falls.

Camera in hand, I'm recording everything
I can't take in—and sit at night or early morning
wordlessly revisiting images, just savoring
the distance, the implicit emotion, the resonance—
that full moon rising over the mountain, the church,
the canyons runneling toward the sea, baptizing us all
with unwonted mystery.

ii
Come day, the harbor gleams below. Above us,
clearly visible, Neruda's home. To reach it we must
cross a canyon, climb a sheer slope. No way but up.
We're always breathless when we get there.
Touring his house, what I envied most was how he,
unquestioningly, set himself at the core of his own world,
a near transparent one, where he feasted his friends,
staged his acquisitions—that carousel horse,
the queen with a ruff, the sole armchair, elaborate bar,
all the epicurean still lives on the narrow stairs
so close you could bite into the fruit, the fish,
as you climbed to reach the pinnacle,
his private panoramic study.

In the bedroom a floor below, a double bed surprisingly
small for such a big-hearted man. Pablo graciously
gave his third wife a third of the wardrobe. Sliding doors
paneled with docile geishas pulled aside revealed
her shoes, neatly paired on the floor, all the same
style but differently dyed, their toes so narrow
they must permanently deform.

The one small dressing table in the corner was preserved,
a sign told us, exactly as it was when she lived there.
Spare. Nothing but a brush. A comb.
The small, hinged mirror angled so she could

always see before being seen. Whitman's portrait
a floor above took up three times the space Pablo
gave her to paint her face.

Did she need those picture windows just as much as he—
even more if she was ever to see herself whole?
Or was this mirror enough, honestly, for both of them?
Could she have needed even less?
Was it enough just to see herself reflected in his eyes?
Was he, charismatic, acquisitive, verbose, loyal, generous,
joyful and libertine, her very own conduit to the infinite?
Why does it pain and liberate me equally
just to think so?

IT IS SO HARD TO LEAVE VALPARAÍSO

It is so hard to leave Valparaíso with its canyons and cerros, the precariously perched, colorful houses, the vivid and ubiquitous murals, the views from our rooftop night and day of sweet plaza Yungay and the alluring sweep of the bay, the heart to hearts with old bronzed poets in the plaza, the lolling sea lions, the waved-dashed cliffs and crowded beach of Playa Ancha, the fearless rope walkers, and the retreats to Viña del Mar with its broader and more pristine beaches, where we leave strange inverted footprints in the sand . . .

It truly is so hard to leave Valparaíso . . . with its endless graffiti and shuttered, plundered stores, the handwritten pleas of shopkeepers to distinguish protest from vandalism, the statues with faces bleeding tears, the elegant four-masted naval schooner that was once a site for torture, our first taste of tear gas, the good humored Uber driver who spun us through coiling back streets our last night, because taxis don't run when there are *manifestaciones*, which he, as do many, defined as a *molestia* (a bother) not a *peligro* (a danger) because they are expressing the discontent of so many in a country where the president's 6% popularity rating is twice that of Congress and three times that of its political parties . . . oh, to leave all this to return to mere impeachment trials and gun rallies . . . pandemics . . . militias . . . marches . . . ever more bitter and elaborated conspiracies . . . wildfires . . . hurricanes . . . floods . . . and my sweet, calm, increasingly surreal daily life . . .

...will be no res...tion.
...o have hunge... all my life for
...herence, co...nuum,
that perf... ...atch between form
and ... ...re, will and acti...
...being invited to da...
...hese dee...ening c...
like a ne... re...
inhib...

THE SPACE BETWEEN NOW & NEVER

WE WRITE TO REDEEM OURSELVES

from the simplest things—rancor,
boredom, bad dreams, the vertigo
of new places we've never yearned for.

I have no more time for ifs or maybes,
wayward empathies, or foreign. It's time
to bring it *all* home—the foregone, forlorn,
forethought, foreclosed, fraught, the knot
in the not.

LIKE A HERMIT CRAB I HAVE DREAMS

of a home that is spacious, fixed
to the earth, a home I can leave
and return to, not a burden
huge and heavy on my own back,
a weight that keeps me constant company,
like an immutable story,
like the sad sighs of my parents
forgotten in their graves,
like the beautiful songs trapped
in the lungs of a deaf mute.
A home I don't need to abandon
to grow, to create.

TOTEMS

I don't know if I chose to absorb them or they
to inhabit me this winter. Some days it feels one way,
some days the other. But they are what I've brought
home with me, duty free: images of pelicans,
grackles, Brahman cattle. They each feel atavistic, necessary.

The pelicans with their ungainly beaks and powerful wings,
starkly silhouetted against the sky—ready to plunge,
hungry, forever hungry, into the foaming sea.
I like the way they surface, gulping, and then cozy in together
on an ocean swell. Each flight triggered independently
by a flash of scale, but in those constantly varying rises
and falls it's like I'm reading music, breathing music,
complex, choral. The only sounds they really make
are like the mysterious grunts of newborn babies dreaming.

And those grackles with that single piercing whistle,
the pause that follows, like someone thrust open
a rusted gate to a magic garden—and paused agog.
The way they perch at sunrise, each on a separate gable,
profiling like vain men. Then fly down and nestle in the palms,
ruffle their necks and loose another sound, more tentative,
a clearing of the throat, a thrum, that entices, endears.
But it's that one wild whistle, the way they release it
and swoop off between buildings, oh, I *wake* for this.
My body hungers to imitate the purity of that sound,
how it surprises itself with its need and its speed.
So very clean—and singular. I like how their whole character
shifts with the rise and fall of the sun, how they become
so deeply social at twilight, their churrs and chatters
filling the air as they settle for the night, by the hundreds,
in the roadside trees, indelibly white-washing
the pavement with their excrement.

I don't know what it is about the Brahmans, only
seen in passing, from a highway or a rutted road,
that makes my heart lurch and ease simultaneously.
There's a poignant gravitas to that high widow's hump,
an extravagance to the vast ruffled fall of skin from chin
to knee—and those drooping ears that seem curved to catch
the sound of blossoms opening, seeds falling, clouds dissolving
along the continental divide, that soft but knowing gleam
in their eyes. A holy empty-mindedness and placidity
that can store and transform sorrow
into a world where the wonder of grass, leaves, forage,
makes life fully worth living. Imagine.

At night I forget all these ideas and just invoke
them, essential, other, silhouetted against the sunset
or the morning sky or a vivid green field, and give
whatever is activated, mysteriously mirrored
in my own brain, my own muscles, free reign.

SCORPIO MOTHERS

i
Down here at the long tail of the continent,
wandering into an art gallery, into a meditation
on maternity, I find a photo that makes me think
of us, sturdy hands against a tapestry ground.
They hold, pincered between thumbs and forefingers,
a large scorpion preserved in a brick of plexiglass.
The gesture is forever ambiguous.
Are the hands pushing away, pulling
near? Is it accusation or source of pride?
No one, truly, loves a scorpion.
But what about us, born under its sign,
with our own roiling, recursive intensities?

You always loved him more, my niece
accuses her mother. Charismatic, beautiful,
hard-working, a passionate protector, a mother
herself, it's only now, in her forties,
her younger brother ten stable years
into a new lease on life, that she can give voice
to this pain. My sister, an unapologetic
Gemini, says brusquely, "Don't you think it's time
you started telling yourself a better story?"

ii
It takes six to seven molts for a scorpion
to mature. To survive, the first molt
must take place riding on her mother's back.
The new exoskeleton is soft, flexible,
but you must keep moving or it will lock you in
tighter than the last one.

I've watched my niece, at home in Brisbane, singing
and dancing with friends to celebrate her own birthday.
How deftly, without losing a beat, she prevents
her adored, mischievous son from picking the cake apart
or blowing out all her candles. "*My* birthday," she says,
catching his hands in both of hers and claiming
with a single breath what's rightfully her own.

His teachers think he is an *enfant terrible*
on the verge of incorrigible—the way he just shared
the razor blades he unscrewed from pencil sharpeners.
A survival skill taught him by his father, Cuban,
who lived through the famines eating cats and guinea pigs.
She tries to explain, pointing out that her son, such
a generous boy, never thought to hoard. He *shared*.
It's illegal, they tell her, even to throw a boomerang here
in Australia. True, their statutes don't explicitly cover
pencil sharpeners, but it's the spirit not
the letter of the law they adhere to.
"My precious boy," she sobs to her mother.
"Why can't they see what I do?"

My heart aches for her, she who shares my sign.
Can we ever really know what story we are living?
Does anything we say or do return to us exactly
as we released it? How often does our greatest
joy arc back to pierce us?

"You can't speed up time. But there are places where it will slow down."

i
Nothing sticks.
I can't remember the opening line
of a poem I wrote yesterday
or the plundered headline
that magnetized the images
in a collage I wove into being hours later
out of images and words I purposefully
diffuse, diffract, and distort
as if I have some control
over the vagaries of my own
mental processing—
more than that, as if I were
on some kind of mystical quest
assured that the prophetic,
the apt but unexpected
will rise to meet me
if I am receptive enough, emptied enough
of preconceptions, hungry enough
for wonder.

ii
At my age, my mother had no idea
who I was, but for the first time
in my forty years appreciated
something about me. I met her there.
Where are we going? she asked me
every five minutes as I drove her
to her first nursing home. Patiently
I repeated, *A new home. A new home.*
Each time she sighed, relaxed.
I kept my eyes on the road, glanced from fields
of artichokes and lettuce on my right,
to the ocean on my left, blinked to hold them
in place, waited for her next question,
felt the valves of my frozen heart
opening again every time I answered,
A place where you'll be safe.

iii
Earlier that year, taking her out to dinner to escape
the chaos she then lived in, she had looked at me
across the table, her hair in wild disarray,
but a colorful coat covering her stained shirt,
her eyes alert, attentive,
her psychiatrist's face in place, benign,
receptive. I knew she would remember
nothing I told her, so I told her everything—
the love affair gone bad I couldn't stop
punishing myself for, the family secrets
I refused to keep, the job where
they wanted to put someone else's name
on my words, my worries about my own
adolescent son. She nodded, asked
appropriate questions. *And then? So?*
How? Why? Whenever I paused,
she would catch my eyes, smile, nod
gently, and I understood something then
about time, forgiveness, memory
that had everything to do with grace
and chance. I wonder now
how long I still have to remember
that moment, to savor the gift that changed
the trajectory of my life. I wonder if I can release
the grief of that question too
into the bottomless well of her attention.

THE SPACE BETWEEN NOW AND NEVER

i
The space between now and never
is hair thin and mesmerizing.
I have no idea why I am telling you this.
I want an old age without mirrors
but with the lithe inner ease
of Moguilevsky's piercing clarinet
inviting me to some way of being
that is incisive and kind
and achingly lyrical.

Is a life that doesn't have *something* deep
and mysterious and absolutely necessary
at its center ever worth living whatever
age you are? *Something* that has nothing
to do with consumption but is all
consuming. The tall window to the street
pulses as if pushed suddenly
by an impatient hand. Nothing in me
shifts in answer. What if it is true
there is nothing else in me urgent
to be known, sown?

ii
The woman alone on the park bench looked up
from her needlepoint as I approached
as if she had expected me, as if the impulse
that felt so strange to me was something
as natural to her as that of a rabbit slipping out
from under a bush, a wild goose changing its position
in a migrating flock, a swan dipping into green water.

"I've never tried this before," she said, holding out
a wooden frame. She meant the photograph
of her own making she had printed on the cloth.
She is stitching in the world around her: the park,
the lake, the birds swooping overhead. A retired biologist,
she now cares for babies and the old and infirm.
Her own children want her to return to Bucharest,
but she sees no reason why they can't meet her where she is,
threading her needle on a bench in El Retiro
on a Saturday afternoon in May,
breathing in springtime, meeting the eyes
of total strangers with the same gentle curiosity
with which she attends to all living things.

There is some profound equipoise within her
and between us as we stand there
looking at her canvas, her first bright stitches.
There is another form of it when she looks up at me
and I, unstoried, fully known, return her smile.
Is this enough?

RESONANCE

i
I'm a night wanderer but I return
in the morning just so we can breathe together,
center in something larger than our own
physiologies. Just this simple skin contact,
these synchronized waves of breath,
and the essential texture of the world
changes. It's so simple and natural, amazing
and magical. No wonder we keep coming back.

These days, perhaps simply as a function of age,
my parasympathetic system is taking over
functions controlled most of my life by fear
and dread and readiness to flee, freeze, fight.
But I'm no stranger to this other state:
this open system, synchronous, receptive, resonant.
It's where I've always gone, alone, to create.

But now it's infusing the world.
An experience I've only had (before you) with children,
especially my own son when he was young.
Or in moments of great change, crises,
when time slows and we know we have become
part of something much larger and are called
to nothing but full presence. Death beds, for example.
They're oddly congenial for me. *Imagination completes
the scene,* Wallace Stevens said. *But in the presence
of extraordinary reality, consciousness takes the place
of imagination.* It's more than consciousness.
We meld with the moment.

ii
Now it's not just in the presence of extraordinary
reality, but on normal days that imagination
and consciousness exchange places.
It reminds me of those days in the late '80s when,
approaching forty, readying myself for whatever
sexual orientation my only son might choose,
I volunteered with young men a few years older than him,
young men dying of AIDS. Those were my own PTSD years,
when no one could get near me physically because
they might haplessly release a truth so terrible *I*
would dissolve, disappear.

They matched me with a young man of twenty-six, high
Anglican, infected his first year at Yale. Jody. I would visit him
at Mass General when he was hospitalized with pneumonia.
His mother, Judy, up from Florida, always pulled her chair
close enough to his bed he was never out of touch.
I would tell them little light stories about my own life,
the deeds and misdeeds of my own mildly rebellious son—
and they would listen entranced, matching mood,
remembering how, only a few years before, their own lives
held the same rhythms, the same tensions, the same
mundane, life-giving hopes.

iii
A year later, in hospice, Jody was in Cheynes-Stokes
breathing, his limbs blue, comatose, but we asked him
to hold on until his mother's plane landed.
It was only a question of an hour or two.
When she arrived, she knelt beside his bed, closed
his hands in hers and cried, "Don't die.
I'll make you French toast in the morning.
Don't go." And something passed between them,
his breathing shifted, began to match hers,
and he held on for another day, another night,
until he was sure she could bear a world
stripped of his breath.

During that day of reprieve, the two us sat together
at either end of his bed, just breathing with him, sharing
observations. The quiet was so deep and sweet.
I can still see Judy's face as she watched him,
a smile playing on her lips. "I wonder what he is
thinking now," she said. "He always had such
a busy mind." But ours weren't busy,
we were just there bathed in the late afternoon sun,
matching breaths with life,
matching breaths with death,
held, we both knew it,
by something more, much more,
than consciousness.

THE DAY I TOOK MY MOTHER TO HER NEW HOME

i
The day I took my mother to her new home—
where the dancer who only spoke word salad
compulsively paced the wood deck
with the insatiable energy of a three year old—
was the day I understood the essential kindness
in my mother. She ignored the haughty widow
of a judge complaining about the servants. Instead
she stood with one foot on the deck, the other
on the dirt path beyond, her hand outstretched,
urging the anxious, hand-wringing dancer to leap
a full six inches to solid ground. "I know you can do it,"
my mother said gently. "I know you can."

That was the day when all the residents paused,
lifted their eyes in unison to the clear blue sky and,
unblinking, watched the long white feathered jet trail
until it completely dissolved . . . just as that day dissolves
almost imperceptibly into this late spring day in December
on the flip side of the globe, where clarinet is fusing
with traffic thrum and inner silence and I am remembering how
only yesterday in the park across from *el ministerio de la defensa,*
on a bench dappled with dancing shadows
from the jacaranda and tipa trees, I mourned
that my camera's screen had gone blank as my mind,
that all my backup images were lost, there was
no track back, that *my* time was coming. I mourned in a way
that did not choose to escape this most terrible of fears:
I too will become one of those on whom *life* is lost.

ii
I remember how, sitting beside me, you maintained that particular
calm you have learned to cultivate whenever you find yourself
in situations you can't control and won't betray, remember it
with the same clarity I remember that morning with my mother
and all the other demented men and women gathered on the deck,
my mother a year younger than I am now, remember how
we all stared steadily skyward, mesmerized,
and I realize now that life *wasn't* lost on any of us,
our breaths found some essential synchrony with each other
and with that slowly dissolving pearl white flume,
the ecstatic slowness of its dispersal,
and the sweetness of that true, annealing blue.

IN THESE DAYS, IN THIS TIME

My heart is now a wall.
Shadows of branches sway across it
making much broader gestures
than in reality.
This is the nature of shadows,
the nature of the heart.

I DON'T WANT TO MOVE ANYTHING FORWARD TODAY

I don't want to move anything forward today.
I just want to memorize my life.
The lone bullfrog's occasional groan,
branches lilting and the leaves
fluttering, green, green, green.
And then this special stillness, unbroken
by the usual morning travails
of our neighbor's laboring hens
loosing eggs I hesitate to eat
they have, descending, so pained
their mothers. But today,
nothing. If the hens have laid,
they've done it silently, painlessly.
Instead I have the piano music drifting in
from the living room, the light lyricism
of Mendelssohn's *Songs Without Words*
shading into something stronger, more insistent,
like occasional rapids in a small forest stream
where the light on the boulders gleams.
I am seventy years old and freed
to receive what I never believed could be.
Completeness.

IT'S TIME TO START TALKING

It's time to start talking without reserve
about all the undeserved
energies inside me fighting
to be received. Sensuality
deeper because it has no
objective correlative. Who would,
seeing me at a distance, ever guess
my own breasts could rest
so gently in my open palms,
my sex could feel so secret
and so wet.

Time has slipped inside my every cell,
etching and curving muscles and skin
in ways that bear no relation to the forces
just as irreversibly shaping my soul.
I never thought ambition would look
like bruises under my eyes, that the creases
between my brows, the gullies on my cheeks
would so firmly contradict
my deepening confidence and eagerness.

There will be no resolution.
I who have hungered all my life for
coherence, continuum,
that perfect match between form
and substance, will and action,
am being invited to dance inside
these deepening contradictions
like a new reality, without
inhibitions, without doubts.

I shout aloud, the windows shake,
and someone I have yet to know
settles herself on the ground of my being,
takes a deep breath, bows to me
as if I were *her* teacher
and pirouettes, leaps, pirouettes,
again again again. I *know*
her every movement from the outside
in and the inside out but something
new has been added, raw, awed, mischievous.
This is just the beginning . . .

WHAT IF

What if these enchanting sunsets
could become a way of life,
a recurrent miracle that never loses
its ability to jolt us into gratitude,
suffuse us with awe, however many times,
however reliably it returns?
What if we never ever grew inured?

By we I mean you and me, the way
standing here together every evening this week,
watching all the diffusions of color
that accompany the slow fall of the sun,
we realize we've entered into a oneness
that feels it can easily last another
twenty-one years. *If we do.*

Faces hold a haunting beauty we were never
alive to before. The light doesn't steadily die out,
instead for a full hour the sky pulses with color,
saffron here, pink there, then plum.
No one wants it to end.
Children throw themselves back into the surf.
Young men catch a last wave. Old men
cast nets. And we, my love, are in the thick of it,
indissolubly one with the wash and the hum.

ALL NIGHT I DREAMT

All night I dreamt about photographing myself
tucked up like an egg. More exactly, a hatchling
on the verge of consciousness, who knows itself best
by the unblemished, translucent shell
that contains it.

We are never too old for rebirth.
Or regress in the service of the whole,
the *hold* of the miraculous.

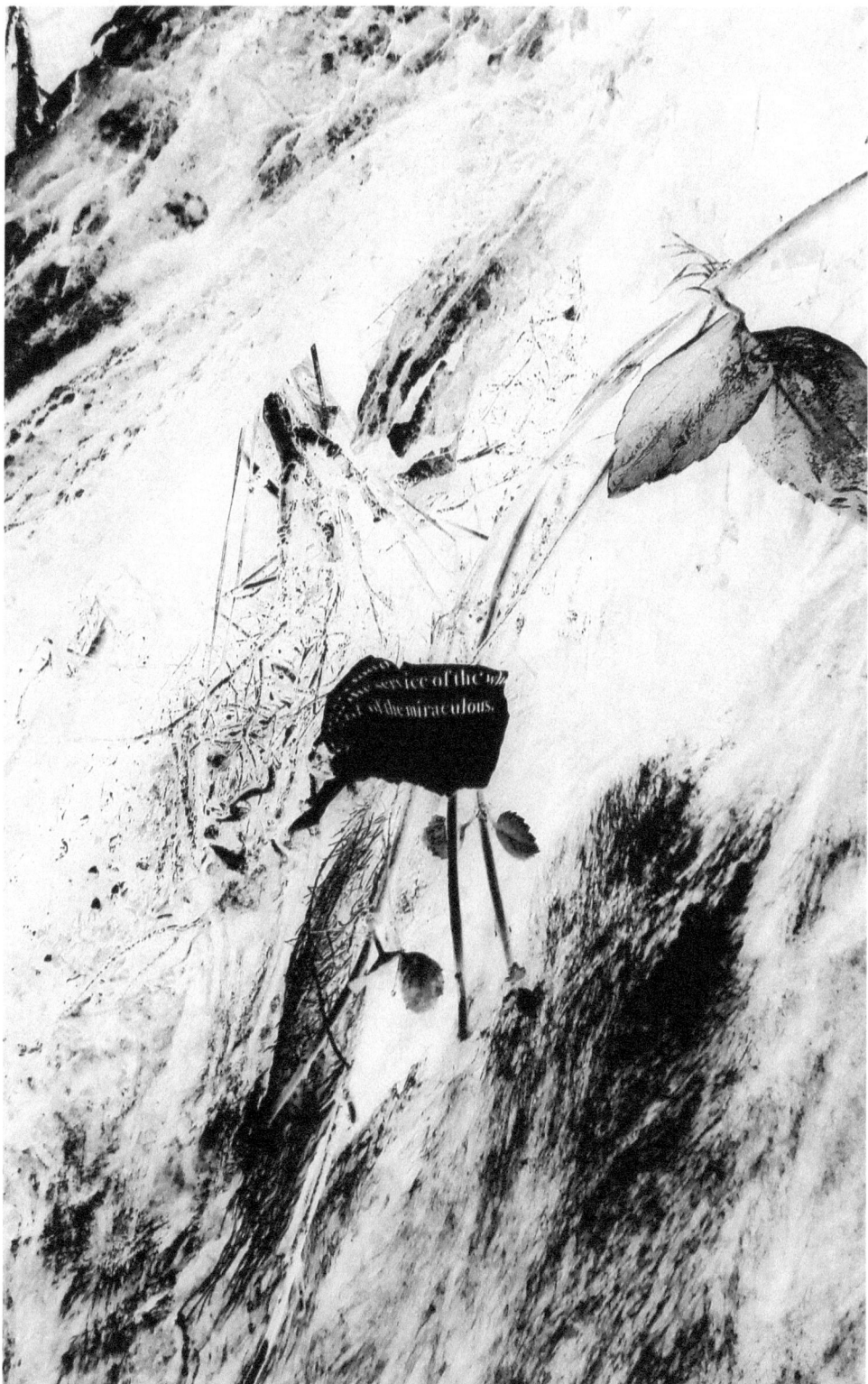

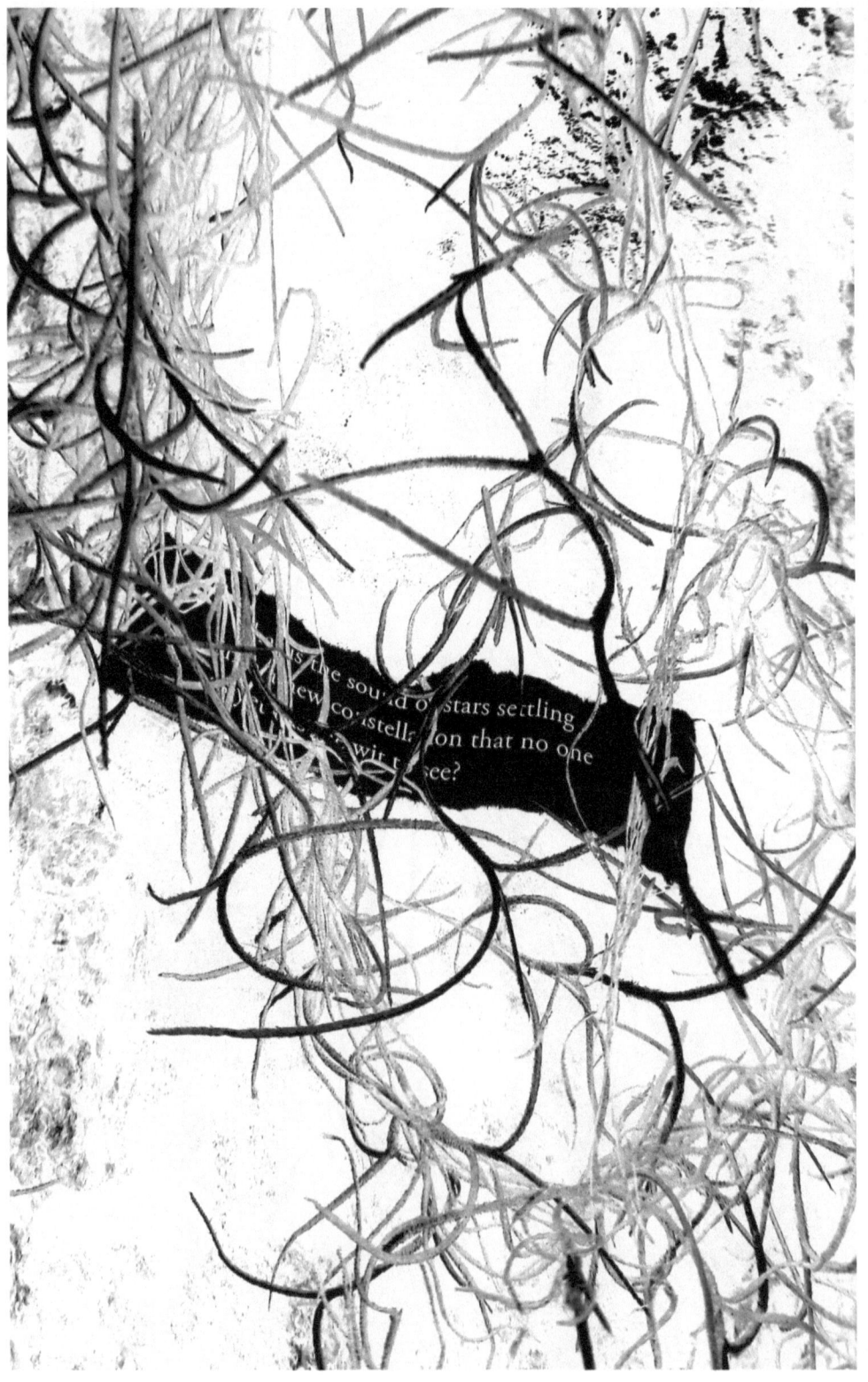

ACKNOWLEDGEMENTS

Special thanks to my very generous and encouraging early readers: Kerry Langan, Michele Markarian, Lilia Trápaga Tenny, and Stephanie Hart. Thanks to all the wonderful members of the Wising Up Press Writers Collective for helping bring the book to print.

The following poems first appeared in Wising Up anthologies: "I Want to Ask Them" and "Accounting" in *Re-Creating Our Common Chord*; "Trust the Emptiness Within" in *Goodness*.

OTHER PUBLICATIONS
Heather Tosteson

Poetry
The Sanctity of the Moment: Poems from Four Decades
Breathing in Portuguese, Living in English

Short Fiction
Hearts as Big as Fists & Other Stories
Germs of Truth

Novels
Visible Signs
The Philosophical Transactions of Maria van Leeuwenhoek, Antoni's Dochter (1668-1696)

Non-Fiction: Wising Up Listening Projects
God Speaks My Language, Can You?

*Sharing the Burden of Repair:
Reentry After Mass Incarceration*

Heather Tosteson is the author of two earlier poetry collections, *The Sanctity of the Moment: Poems from Four Decades* and *Breathing in Portuguese, Living in English*, as well as several works of fiction and non-fiction. She is the recipient of fellowships in poetry, fiction, and photography from Yaddo, MacDowell, the Virginia Center for the Creative Arts, and Hambidge Center for the Arts as well as a Discovery/The Nation poetry prize. A co-founder of Wising Up Press, she has co-edited and illustrated sixteen Wising Up Anthologies. She earned her MFA in Creative Writing from the University of North Carolina in Greensboro and PhD in English and Creative Writing from Ohio University.

www.ingramcontent.com/pod-product-compliance
Lightning Source LLC
Chambersburg PA
CBHW030854170426
43193CB00009BA/604